From Nowhere to Somewhere

How a Small-Town Dreamer Became an Oxbridge Scholar

The ultimate guide to earning a place at the universities of Oxford and Cambridge

Dr Julian Tan L. Y.

BA MEng (Oxon), PhD (Cantab)

CW01499366

From Nowhere to Somewhere

To my parents, Patrick and Yeen, who've supported me every step of the way and encouraged me to pursue my dreams. You're the driving force behind everything I've accomplished. To my brother, Jesper, who's always been by my side, shielding me and keeping me grounded. And to my best friend, Jasper, for your endless optimism and for constantly pushing me to reach higher.

Contents

Introduction

I grew up an ambitious kid. I always had goals I'd strive for. I'd write them down on strips of paper using the nicest marker I could find in my family's stationery box, a repurposed Danish biscuit tin housing stray pencils, pens, and markers we collected over time.

These goals were all shapes and sizes. Sometimes they were small, like 'do thirty push-ups' or 'complete revision of chapters 4 and 5'. Sometimes they were bigger, like 'be first in class in Additional Mathematics, Biology, and Chemistry' or 'win the state Physics Championship'. But there was always one goal, the ultimate goal that guided me throughout my entire growing-up years – to 'Get into a top university'. This was my North Star, my compass.

I can't quite put my finger on when exactly this goal came to be but getting into a top university was my number one priority. I saw it as a golden ticket to a transformed life, a silver bullet that would change the trajectory of my life.

I grew up in a middle-class family in a suburban town in Malaysia. That town, Subang Jaya, recently received 'city' status. But when I grew up, it was an oil-palm estate that had just been redeveloped into a residential area containing rows and rows of terraced and semi-detached houses in clusters numerically coded under the heading of 'USJ'. I grew up in 'USJ 5'. It was a sleepy, unremarkable town.

And perhaps it was exactly for that reason that I yearned for more. I was lucky enough to have great parents who instilled in me the importance of education. They both grew up poor but made the life they had by each taking a one-way air ticket to the United Kingdom for college. My dad sold his motorcycle to fund his plane ticket and held multiple jobs to pay for the fees and expenses (back in those days, one could do this, but not anymore!). He did everything from teaching taekwondo to flipping burgers in a diner – the very same diner where he met my mom, who was washing the dishes.

Their time spent in England was transformative not only because they met each other there but also because it was a key turning point in their lives. They were able to get good jobs when they returned to Malaysia with degrees from England that laid the foundation for the life they built for me and my brother. So, education was always central in our household.

Granted, I don't think my parents extolled education to a much higher degree than a typical Asian family. It's widely known that Asian parents sometimes tend to take a proactive, even aggressive, approach to education for their children, for the same reason my parents instilled its importance in me.

But what was different was that I understood its power. I understood its power beyond merely revising for the sake of getting an 'A' or making my parents happy by being an obedient son. I understood the power of education in a way that even now I'm surprised at how I knew what I knew.

I saw it as 'hope', an abstract light that not only served the purpose of intellectual pursuit. It was a ticket to a life I couldn't yet fathom as a kid but knew that that life was a much better one than the one I was living at the time.

This deep understanding and desire ultimately led me to articulate my North Star goal of getting into a top university, a radical goal for me.

You must understand that the schools I went to growing up didn't churn out Ivy League students. The high school I went to was a government school, where one of the girls in my year got pregnant at the age of sixteen. It was a school riddled with bullying problems and one where I was often the target thanks to my

3

penchant for learning and inclination to pursue education in a serious manner.

So, even to have the courage to articulate a dream this big was, and remains, one of the boldest things I've done.

I'd pore over the Times University Rankings every year to see the movements within the top ten universities. Harvard, Oxford, Cambridge, Stanford, Yale – these were all schools I grew up looking up to, never imagining that I'd one day be so lucky as to spend my most formative years learning in not one but two of them and benefiting from the best education this world could offer.

I got into the University of Oxford on a partial scholarship to read Engineering, Economics and Management as an undergraduate, and then was offered a full scholarship to pursue a PhD in Materials Engineering at the University of Cambridge. To be one of the few Malaysians to have ever done the Oxbridge 'double', I know how incredibly privileged I was.

I still remember the moment I received the email from the University of Oxford informing me that they were extending an offer to me to join their esteemed university. The level of joy was ethereal, other-worldly. I remember jumping up and down as if I could take flight. The rest of my memory from that evening largely draws a blank but it was the best night of my life.

I'm acutely aware that to some people this may not be that big a deal. Getting into a top university for some is their expectation and a rite of passage.

But to me it was a big deal – it was the culmination of all my years of setting a goal, working towards it, and finally seeing it come to fruition against so many odds. It felt impossible until it became a reality.

All I had was a dream and years of subconscious and conscious preparation. To see it realised was an incredible feeling. And then to convert the opportunity I had at Oxford to get into Cambridge was another life-defining moment.

I've come to reflect on everything I did that helped me realise my dreams of getting into a top university – as they say, hindsight is 20/20. I've also had the benefit of gaining insight from my Oxbridge peers and their own squiggly paths to their dream universities. Adding that to the teaching experience I had at Cambridge when I was doing my PhD, I learnt a lot about what top institutions really look for in their students.

I'll share in this book everything I know.

I'll share personal stories and anecdotes to bring the lessons I've learnt to life. I want this book to be an easy read that tackles the crux of the issues in a way that feels grounded and relevant to you, the reader.

The truth is, even though it's been more than a decade since I stepped foot into the hallowed grounds of the University of Oxford as a green, naive, bespectacled teen, getting into Oxford changed my life.

Being in the company of high intellect and incredibly talented individuals, the rigorous academic environment, quaint traditions and, most of all, the exposure to opportunities I uniquely had access to solely because I was at Oxbridge, broadened my horizons enormously. So much so that I continue to see my life as a life of two parts – the first being 'pre-Oxbridge' and the second, 'post-Oxbridge'.

By being an Oxford graduate, I had prestigious companies across the spectrum knocking on my door, trying to recruit me. I had a growing network of influential people I could call friends and schoolmates. I gained access to an alumni network of amazing people doing amazing things who shared a common past with me – one that was so embedded in our identities that they'd look out for me and push that little bit more for me just because we had the same alma mater.

But, most of all, I matured in a high-performance environment that set me up with good habits that laid the foundations for a robust career and fulfilling life. And then to complete the Oxbridge portmanteau by being accepted into the University of Cambridge cemented my access into incredible opportunities I continue to enjoy to this day.

They say, 'education is an investment'. What they imply but don't explicitly say is that '*good* education is a *lucrative* investment'.

Sure, getting into a top university requires investing time, effort, and, not to mention, money – studying at a top university doesn't come cheaply. But my years of preparation that enabled me to realise my ultimate dream have paid off handsomely.

Financially, I was earning six figures (in British pounds) less than three years after leaving Oxbridge. I enjoyed an accelerated career, making it into the leadership teams at Formula 1 and a FTSE 20 global entertainment company as one of the youngest members by far in both scenarios. I have an incredible network of friends and colleagues who've founded multimillion-pound businesses, are heirs to multibillion-pound businesses, some are finding the cure for cancer, and others are shaping political agendas and national policies. But, above all, I have an unshakeable sense of security in my career and life that I can confidently attribute to being able to be called an Oxford and Cambridge graduate. No matter what happens, I'm an Oxbridge graduate and that will always hold tremendous value to unlock whatever opportunity I choose to pursue.

Getting into Oxbridge is very achievable with the right preparation and guidance. This book provides lessons, tips, and advice that, coupled with preparation, will help you realise your dream of attending your top university.

And if Oxbridge isn't your goal, just replace 'Oxbridge' with the name of any other top university you may aim for. Heck, 'Oxbridge' can be replaced by any ambitious goal you may have in life.

The ingredients of success transcend all pursuits and that's what makes life both hard and easy at the same time. Hard because the ingredients themselves require investment, commitment, and focus; easy because, once you've learnt the tricks, it's just a case of 'rinse and repeat'.

My hope is that the guidance in this book will empower you to achieve your dreams, whether they involve Oxbridge, any other dream university, or any goal that drives you forward in life. Now, let's dive into the book and help turn your ambitions into reality.

Part 1

The Building Blocks

1
Be curious

When growing up, I was taught always to ask 'Why'. Why was the sky blue during the day but orange at dusk? Why was there no snow (in Malaysia where I grew up) during Christmas like in the movies? Why would placing a magnifying glass over a newspaper during a sunny day set it alight?

My parents would encourage me to explore the world through an unending string of whys. Each why was a shovel unearthing new insights and facts. I'd turn to my father as a little kid and ask him, 'Why did I have to go to bed before everyone else?'

He'd answer, 'Because you need at least eight hours of sleep.'

I'd ask, 'Why do I need eight hours of sleep? Why couldn't I just have five?'

'Because you need eight hours of sleep to grow big and strong.'

'Why do I need to be big and strong?'

'Because being big and strong gives you advantages – nobody will want to pick on you if you're big and strong.'

'But why would people want to pick on me in the first place?'

And it would go on and on.

Looking back, I have to acknowledge how patient my parents were in weathering my barrage of questions. They didn't always have the answers and my father, I'd later learn, would very often just conjure up convincing-sounding answers to placate my intrigue. But their sheer ability, willingness and even enthusiasm to support and cultivate my occasionally annoying curiosity laid the foundations for my future success.

It's because of my curiosity that I knew the sky changed colour due to the way sunlight refracts through the atmosphere. Or why consistent solar heating near the equator overrides influences that drive the four seasons. Or in the context of convex lenses what a focal point is.

I'd find myself in situations where I'd know why things were the way they were without having been formally taught about them in school. And this made all the difference.

My favourite TV show by far was *Bill Nye, The Science Guy*, a brilliant series about a scientist named Bill who would investigate the wonderful world around us through experiments, utilising everyday materials in an attempt to explain phenomena in the simplest terms.

I learnt what a dicotyledon was at the age of six by growing some dried mung beans on damp cotton pads before formally learning about them in school at the age of twelve. I learnt about centripetal forces when I was seven through an experiment spinning a bucket full of water without any spillage, only learning that physics concept years later when I was thirteen.

Because of my curiosity, I was often ahead of my class in a lot of things. I had a penchant for more quantitative subjects, such as mathematics and science, and consistently aced my academics that further strengthened my confidence to push for greater academic excellence. My curiosity created a virtuous cycle of curiosity converting into competence and then confidence, leading to more curiosity. This built the core of my academic success that allowed me to realise my ultimate dream of getting into top universities, such as Oxford and Cambridge.

I was always effortlessly one or two steps ahead of everyone else in my class. And not only was I accelerating my learning process by cultivating my own curiosity, but I was finding immense joy in immersing myself in the rich wonders of this world, a world full of curious things.

I saw science as a form of magic, a way to manifest my imagination into reality. Studying chemistry to me was the real-world analogue of studying potions at Hogwarts, physics classes were like charms practice, and biology (at least on the plant side), herbology. As a kid, you can only imagine how riveting and engrossing having that mindset was to me.

And I'm a big believer in finding joy in everything that you're doing (more on that in a later chapter). Curiosity was just a key to unlock the joy and fascination that were already there.

Top universities such as Oxbridge look for curious students. This is not a hunch – it's a fact. Meet any alumnus and you'll find that being curious oftentimes comes out as one of their top attributes.

Oxbridge professors interviewing students applying for spots in their coveted institutions are looking for curiosity when they interview.

I remember when preparing for my own Oxford interview, one of the top tips I read was to show curiosity in the interviews. I thought to myself, 'Well that's easy. I'll just be myself.' And that was exactly what I did. I leaned into my natural state as a result of cultivating this trait and the interview was one of the most fun conversations I'd ever had. It clearly worked because I was one of the five Malaysians that year who were offered a spot at Oxford.

The reality of the Oxbridge interviews is that you won't know the answer to every question. Forget the interview – life is full of unanswered questions. But what the professor or interviewer is trying to distil from those forty-five-minutes-to-an-hour's conversation with you is how capable you'll be at finding answers and solutions to questions you don't know the answers or solutions to. And, let me tell you, having curiosity means the difference between being able to crack a hard problem and being cracked by a hard problem.

Curiosity is also prized in top universities such as Oxbridge because curious students are able to thrive under high pressure and ambiguous situations with less effort. This is because either they're quite a bit ahead in terms of what they already know or they have a greater confidence in solving problems themselves by being armed with their superpower – curiosity.

Having been to both Oxford and Cambridge, I can tell you the environment is challenging – academically, mentally, emotionally. You're in an environment with the world's best talent, each being top students in their respective high schools before transitioning to university. Each with a big brain and oftentimes even a bigger ego. It's highly competitive being there, and the ability to thrive rests on the finest of margins.

Having curiosity is a prerequisite. It's not optional.

And the thing about curiosity is that it can be learnt. It's one of the most powerful tools I believe we all have access to but only a small proportion tap into.

The key is to take a genuine interest in the things that surround you. Taking the time to be present in the moment to comprehend the intricacies of even the most seemingly mundane of things. Leave behind any expectations you may have about the usefulness or purpose of questioning things for that moment. Just comprehend things for what they are and you'll find that your natural instinct to start questioning why things are the way they are will start to emerge.

If you're in a park, reading this book on a glorious, sunny day, you might start to feel the warmth of the sunlight kissing your skin by just taking the moment to be present. And by taking an interest, you might start to wonder why and how sunlight transmits heat.

Or if you're reading this in your bedroom just before you go to sleep, you might start to wonder why people like to read before they sleep. Does it help them sleep or is it because it's a natural gap in the day to read?

With the world's vast information literally at our fingertips thanks to the advent of the internet, mobile phones, Google and, more recently, AI chatbots, the answers to any questions you might have can easily be accessed. If science was magic like chemistry was potions, the internet has to be the ultimate form of wizardry. I remember when I grew up before the internet was established, I'd pore over encyclopaedias for answers – those hardcover publications, each at least two to three inches thick and covering a few parts of the alphabet at a time. I swiftly transitioned to Microsoft *Encarta* when that was launched as the first digitised version of the encyclopaedia – many of you reading will never even have heard of *Encarta* but if your curiosity is starting to grow, you might just Google it.

The beauty of cultivating curiosity is that it's a self-reinforcing endeavour. The more curious you are about something, the more you'll seek answers to questions. And the more you seek answers to questions, the more you'll realise how little you know or understand about the world – which in turn will make you want to learn more.

As the German-American poet and novelist Charles Bukowski once famously said, 'Intelligent people are full of doubts, while the stupid ones are full of confidence.'

There's truth in this and, while this presents a different sort of problem for the world, it captures the essence of the point I want to make about how curiosity spurs intelligence and creates a virtuous cycle for greater intelligence.

It's no secret that getting into a top university such as Oxford or Cambridge requires intellect. And so, if intellect is the foundation of an aspiring student's application, curiosity is the brickwork on which that intellect is built.

Keep asking 'why'. Keep asking 'what if'. Allow your imagination to run wild. Keep doing that until it becomes a habit, until it becomes second nature to you. And you'll have developed a strong foundation on which to build your Oxbridge dreams.

2
Dream big

Everything starts with a dream. The ability to visualise something that's not yet a reality has to be one of the greatest distinguishing drivers for the success of the human race. All great inventions and achievements, from air travel to the internet to landing on the moon, started with a dream, a vision for articulating the art of the possible.

As a kid, my dream was to get into a top university. I saw it as a golden ticket that would transform my life. To me this was a huge dream because I didn't grow up in an environment where going to university was a given, let alone to an overseas university, and, what's more, a prestigious one. The high school I went to was a state school that was riddled with issues from bullying to underperformance, and there was a dearth of real-life role models. Students there generally didn't care much about education and many would forgo tertiary education altogether, sometimes by necessity and at other times by choice.

So, for me to be able to dream of getting into a top university was a pretty unusual, and quite frankly scary, thing. But I'll for ever be grateful that I dreamt that big. Without a doubt, I credit my acceptance at the universities of Oxford and Cambridge, and every success that I've experienced since then – from being able to build a successful career in London to securing complete financial freedom for myself and my family – to that one dream.

My decision to visualise and vocalise this ambitious goal meant the difference between merely settling with what I had and striving for so much more.

As I look back, my courage to dream that big probably came from a combination of factors.

First, the importance of education was instilled in me early on by my parents. They were always big on education because they experienced firsthand how having access to a good education changed their own outlooks on their lives. My father grew up very poor. He'd tell me stories of him frequenting temples as a child to get fed because there wasn't any food at home. Or how once a year, during the Lunar New Year, his late mom, my late grandmother, would treat the family with pig's ears stewed in sweet soy sauce – scraps that she'd procure cheaply from the local butcher. It was when my father sold everything he had, for that one-way plane ticket to England to become a student, that his life turned around. He built upon that an impressive career in Sales and

Marketing, ultimately becoming Managing Director of the South-East Asian and Chinese markets for a major consumer goods company. This allowed him to provide me and my brother a sheltered upbringing.

Second, I made a decision very early on to be fearless when I set my goals. I'm not sure where this confidence (or arrogance) came from if I'm honest, but to me goals and dreams were always meant to be aspirational and ambitious in nature. They were meant to be a target to focus your energy and spirit on so that as you strove for that goal, even if you fell short, you'd still land an amazing position because you dreamt big enough.

I later came across a wonderful quote by Liberian politician Ellen Johnson Sirleaf that said, 'If your dreams don't scare you, they're not big enough.' Those words perfectly embody the very essence of my approach to dreaming big.

Third, it takes the same amount of effort to dream big as to dream small, practically speaking. So, why limit your dreams when you can have dreams of any size for virtually the same amount of effort?

I've seen time and again that many young teens let assumptions, fears, and doubts shrink their ambitions. Many just conclude that they're not Oxbridge material or that getting into a top university is impossible because the admission rates are so low. They convince themselves that they won't be able to get in and ultimately write the ending to their own story without allowing that 1 per cent chance to breathe. They're too afraid to dream that big maybe because they're afraid of failure, of standing out from the crowd, or of being laughed at.

I think it's fundamentally important to stamp out these fears. There are a lot of things in this life that you're not in control of, but one thing you are in control of is the narrative you tell yourself and the standards you set for yourself. Take full control of those and be the captain of your own ship and the author of your own story.

Dreaming big is about allowing yourself to stretch beyond your known boundaries, to strive for much more than you think you're capable of so that you can force growth. It allows you to manifest something lofty and grow it into existence.

You've picked up this book, which is a strong mark of intent from you to realise your dream of getting into Oxford, Cambridge, or any other top university. Believe this is possible because it's what you want for yourself, stepping out of what might feel safe and comfortable to you.

And once you've done that, write it down. Yes, write your big dream down in your best handwriting on a sheet of paper.

I'm a big believer in cultivating accountability, momentum, and, ultimately, belief through verbalising one's own dreams and goals. When I set the goal of getting into a top university, I didn't just keep that to myself as an abstract idea in my head. Using my nicest marker, I wrote it down on a strip of paper so that I could see the goal, touch it, and be regularly reminded of it. I stuck it on the plastered wall in front of my bedroom table, which was the most visible part of my room so that every morning when I woke up I'd see it. Every time I looked up when I was revising for my exams in my bedroom, I'd see it. Every time I was about to switch off the lights to go to bed, I'd see it.

The more I saw it, the more achievable my dream seemed to me and the less scary it became.

I'd also start to vocalise this dream to the closest people around me whom I could trust. These were people like my parents whom I knew would support me and help me build my own self-belief.

This not only allowed me to share the weight of my big dream, but it also created accountability and ownership, which were, in hindsight, incredibly important elements.

It became *my* dream, *my* ambition, so much so that it almost intertwined with my identity and the way I saw myself. It created momentum and inspiration for me that helped me through times when doubts crept in.

And, make no mistake, there will be many doubts, many lows on your own journey. You may flunk a test or you may be scoffed at for daring to dream that big or you may just get tired of running so fast for so long. I went through all of that. I was even bullied at high school for being a 'nerd' but I never lost sight of my ultimate goal. Having it written down and clearly articulated on my bedroom wall was a key part of the solution – it was like having a secret incantation that always brought me back to the centre when things pushed me to stray away.

They say the best plans are always written down. Think about the number of times you were far more productive just because you had written down a to-do list.

Writing down goals and intent makes them real. So, if you're reading this right now, I hope I've convinced you first to be brave and tell yourself you'll set an ambitious goal to get into Oxbridge. And then write it down! Write it down in big bold letters with the best pen or marker you have and stick it somewhere prominent for you to come back to constantly. Start to share your dreams with people who'll support you, and only people who'll support you. It goes without saying – don't bother sharing your big dreams with people who might have even the slightest doubts. They're not ready for you and you shouldn't waste time on them (more on this in a later chapter). Your big dream is incredibly precious. Protect and nurture it as you would your own loved one or most prized possession.

Because daring to dream big is not an easy endeavour, and your ability to get into Oxbridge starts with believing that getting there lies within your realm of possibilities.

Your biggest limiting factor is usually your own imagination, not your ability. Remember Ellen Johnson Sirleaf's wise words – if your dreams don't scare you, they're not big enough!

3

Do things you don't like doing

We all have natural inclinations. While some of them are nurtured through the environment we grow up in, others are by nature genetically coded into our personal database since birth.

Some of us may prefer more pensive, introspective activities such as reading, meditating, and art, while others may have a penchant for more adrenaline and exhilaration, enjoying the rugged outdoors or occasional roller-coaster rides.

Whatever your natural (or taught) inclination is, I'm here to encourage you to do things you don't think you'd like doing. Do things outside your comfort zone if you want to get into Oxbridge.

I've been an introvert for as long as I can remember. I've always preferred more solitary, contemplative activities. I'm much more comfortable picking up a paintbrush and swiping watercolour paint on to a canvas or when I was kid, reading Enid Blyton books alone in my bedroom. So, people always found it surprising when I told them that this reserved kid also possessed an upper brown belt in taekwondo.

For those of you who aren't familiar with taekwondo, an upper brown belt is just one rung below black-belt level, the most advanced belt rank. The truth is that in spite of what my advanced belt colour might suggest, I hated taekwondo. I don't use the word 'hate' lightly or often. There are very few things in life I'd say I've hated but I really didn't enjoy taekwondo.

It was entirely because of my dad that I picked up martial arts in the first place. I'd wake up very early every Saturday morning, put on my taekwondo uniform and head for training. We'd perform endless sets of punches, front kicks, side-kicks, and roundhouse kicks against leather-skinned pads that we'd hold up for each other to beat into submission. And then we'd transition to learning a fixed set of moves in a routine called *taegeuk* (required for passing one's taekwondo exams) before finishing up the lesson by sparring with a partner and then heading home to do another two hours of training with my dad and the sandbag he'd installed at the back of our house.

As someone who prefers diplomatic reconciliation over physical confrontation, I can tell you that taekwondo (and particularly the sparring sessions) was not my idea of fun on a Saturday. But my father was and continues to be deeply passionate about martial arts – he has a second-dan black belt – and I'm very grateful he made me take up taekwondo. It gave me self-confidence and toughened me up in ways only knowing how to throw a kick could do. I also learnt more about myself: that I lean more towards being a pacifist and that I could flex way beyond my own comfort zone and still excel even if I had zero natural inclination (or talent, for that matter) in those areas.

There are many other things I forced myself to take up and stick to doing, in the name of self-discovery and stepping outside my comfort zone. From becoming a Scout and earning my Tenderfoot badge to training for squash and representing my school at the state championships to even walking down the runway for L'Oréal, I made sure I didn't close myself off to experiences that, on paper, I might have perceived as 'not being my cup of tea'.

This helped me acquire a broad range of experiences, some directly beneficial to my application to Oxbridge, such as the extracurricular activities I undertook, some indirectly beneficial such as the broader experiences that helped me mature my thinking and approach to life.

The key to all of this is to do things that are uncomfortable for you, not for anybody else. Do them for yourself, because you recognise there's always something you can learn from stepping outside what feels comfortable. Don't do them just because your parents asked you to, or because this book is encouraging you to.

Because if the motivation for putting yourself out there comes from external sources, it won't last. You'll tire out. It will be a favour you're doing for somebody else when really it should be something you do for your own learning and development.

While my father did make me take up taekwondo when I was five, it was my decision to stick with it for as long as I did as a teen because I saw tremendous value in it. The same for Scouts, squash, and modelling. My parents never pressured me to continue doing things if I decided I didn't want to – it was always my decision to make. Which is why I stopped taekwondo at upper brown belt instead of making it to black belt or why I stopped being a Scout after earning my Tenderfoot badge. What my parents did brilliantly, though, was to cultivate in me an open mind, encouraging me to try things at least twice to see if I'd enjoy them.

This openness to explore is now a central philosophical tenet in my life and has led me to new experiences that have only broadened my own horizons. I believe this is a distinguishing factor for my success in getting into Oxbridge.

The truth is, discomfort is really just a sign of growth. When you hit the gym and work your muscles for the first time, you'll be familiar with the pain and aches that follow – this is just a sign of your muscles recovering, strengthening, and growing. Or remember how uncomfortable the experience was when you picked up a new sport for the first time, realising perhaps that you lacked basic hand–eye coordination like I did. For me, it was missing the rubber ball with every swing the first time I picked up a racquet and stepped into a squash court. That discomfort, stemming from embarrassment was a sign of my learning, of my growing.

We all tend to gravitate towards what feels comfortable and familiar. It's human nature. Feeling comfortable satisfies our deep-seated evolutionary need to feel safe and secure. This warm feeling of safety is what we have evolved to chase after, because it indicates a lack of threats to our own survival.

But we no longer live in caves like we used to, fighting for our survival against sabre-tooth tigers or woolly mammoths. We can afford to push ourselves outside our comfort zones more.

Not only will this broaden our horizons, but it will also help us become more empathetic and understanding of differences if we put ourselves in new and unfamiliar circumstances.

Having empathy and emotional intelligence is a valuable prerequisite for gaining admission to a top university such as Oxford or Cambridge, where the best students from across the world assemble in a single lecture hall. Being able to appreciate differences because you can see from other people's perspectives will allow you to learn from this rich diversity of thought. Top universities look for this in their students to ensure a productive learning environment for everyone.

Doing things you don't like doing and stepping outside your comfort zone will be hard at first but, like anything, it becomes easier with repetition. It's so encoded in my being now that even when it comes to trying unusual foods, I'm totally open to it – from happily trying deep-fried grasshoppers in the street markets of Beijing to sampling fermented shark meat in Iceland. Yum!

I think it's important to put preconceived notions and other people's judgements aside, so you can come to your own conclusions on things. And it's worth it to put in that extra effort to do things you don't like because you realise how much better equipped you become to deal with the diversity of challenges that life will inevitably throw at you. All this builds on your repertoire of experiences and strengthens your own case for being admitted into Oxbridge.

Because doing things that you don't like doing fundamentally signals an openness for learning. And top universities like Oxbridge are looking for mouldable students who are open to and have a deep hunger for learning about everything this wonderful world can offer us.

4

Do well the things you like

If the advice from the previous chapter is to do lots of things you don't like, then what about the things you do like?

As mentioned earlier, we all have natural tendencies and inclinations. There will always be certain things that will come as second nature to us. For me, the thing that came naturally was science. Since a very early age, I was glued to science programmes on TV, my favourite by far, as mentioned before, being *Bill Nye, the Science Guy*. Bill, an American mechanical engineer turned TV presenter, conducted simple and wacky scientific experiments, aimed at kids to explain the interesting phenomena happening in the world around us.

It was enthralling and, as a kid with a curious imagination who devoured the Harry Potter books when they came out, science was to me the real-world equivalent of witchcraft and wizardry. I took to it super easily and spent a lot of time conducting my own scientific experiments at home as I also pored over my school curriculum for Physics, Chemistry, and Biology.

The ability to lean into my hunger for learning about science was a huge contributing factor to my admission into the University of Oxford to study engineering. Science was something I immensely enjoyed and hence spending copious amounts of time on it came simply and allowed me to build excellence in it.

I found joy in learning about everything from Newton's laws of motion to the concept of the conservation of energy and even learning about Einstein's theory of relativity at the age of nine. It created a virtuous cycle. The more I learnt, the more I enjoyed knowing and the more I wanted to continue levelling up my knowledge. As a result, school was never too difficult for me and the academic accolades I racked up were instrumental in my application to Oxford.

Now, you might say, 'What if I don't like chemistry or physics?' My response to that is to find a subject you do enjoy. The wonderful thing about primary and secondary education is that we're exposed to a broad range of subjects from a young age. From history and art to languages and mathematics, there's bound to be a subject that resonates with you, especially if you're curious about the world per my advice earlier in this book.

Lean into that subject and use that natural inclination you have for it as fuel to build excellence, competence, and confidence. Then, when the time comes for you to apply to Oxbridge or any other top university, you'd have strengthened a natural muscle into becoming a superpower that the institutions just won't be able to ignore.

Ultimately, I'm a big believer in peaking on your strengths while just being good enough in your areas of weakness. This is a winning formula not just for getting into Oxbridge but for any aspect of life. It ensures you're constantly levelling up your strengths, which will serve as your clear defining features, while ensuring your areas for development don't hold you back.

Deeply reflect on what topics or activities interest and inspire you. This may require you to be open-minded and curious and may take time, requiring self-awareness too. Allow yourself that space and time. After all, whatever area you decide to lean into could very well shape how you live the rest of your life. Spending a few months or years to try new things and discover hidden passions is what your early years are for. Join that maths club or pick up that hockey stick. Do an internship or start building that lemonade stand.

Once you learn more about yourself, start leaning into those productive areas that you genuinely enjoy. Build that virtuous cycle with the goal to be the best in the world at it so that when it comes to applying to your dream university, it will not only be obvious what subject you should be pursuing but it will also give your application a boost through your strong track record in excelling in that subject. For me, I was able to prove my strong interest in engineering through the state and district championships I'd won in physics and mathematics and, of course, my grades were more than in order.

The other advice I'd give you is to concentrate your efforts in a small number of areas rather than spreading yourself too thinly. While there's tremendous value in acquiring a broad range of experiences, make sure you catch yourself before this comes at the expense of having an impact on your ability to peak in your strengths.

I could have gone for that black belt in taekwondo or pursued my path to becoming a King Scout, but we all have only twenty-four hours in a day. So, I made the decision to lean into my natural strengths of science and mathematics as I grew in my teens to ensure I could go deep enough into those areas, rather than go too broadly.

Put in the long hours to develop your understanding and skills in the subjects you like. And find ways to take your interests to a more advanced level, such as teaching others, taking on leadership roles, or pursuing your own independent research outside the school curriculum.

I regularly used to teach my classmates the scientific theories and concepts we had to learn in school, in part because we didn't always have access to the best teachers, and in part, because I felt that my own understanding of those topics significantly improved when I taught my peers. This was because it required me to explain complex concepts in the simplest of terms. As Einstein once said, 'If you can't explain it simply, you don't understand it well enough.'

I also took on multiple leadership positions at school, such as being the president of multiple societies, honing my relevant skills. And I spent countless hours outside school conducting my own scientific experiments in the name of fun and subconsciously upskilling my own competence.

Joining a top university is about getting the best education this world can offer on a subject of your choosing. You're being taught the most complex and intellectually challenging things in that pursuit of knowledge.

As a consequence, being able to demonstrate both your expertise and passion through your achievements reassures those admitting you that you have what it takes not only to survive the gruelling course at Oxbridge, but will thrive when times get tough (and they do get tough, even for the brightest students).

So, do the things you like well, and use this as a strong foundation for your application to Oxbridge. After all, what's better than pursuing what you love and being great at it, all the while having the power of a top university behind you to propel your performance into the stratosphere?

5
Pick your friends wisely

I've been given a lot of different advice throughout the years, but none as impactful as the one my parents gave me when they sat me down before I started school.

Both my father and mother were working parents. Hailing from the resilient baby-boomer generation, they emerged from humble beginnings, their lives transformed through the pursuit of education and their relentless dedication to building their careers.

And so, I hardly saw them as a child. I'd occasionally see my father for breakfast before the school bus arrived in the early hours of dawn. And after school, I'd be on my own watching TV and doing a bit of homework before he came home just as I'd change into my pyjamas to go to bed. I'd see my mom even less because she worked in the city (Kuala Lumpur, the capital of Malaysia). From where we lived, with the heavy Malaysian traffic, it could take between two and sometimes three-and-a-half hours on a bad day to complete the trip, so she always came home late and also left for work early.

Perhaps it's because of their absence in my formative years that they felt it important to sit me down when I was six to ingrain in me the importance of picking my circle of friends. Because of how busy both my parents were – they knew that I'd be spending the majority of my time with my friends in school – they were keen to ensure I grew up in the right environment.

I was only six, but I remember it like it was just yesterday, how my parents sat me down on the Sunday evening before school opened. They said to me, 'Ju, make sure you pick your friends wisely. You'll be a reflection of them, if not now, eventually.'

Those words struck me like a lightning bolt. So much wisdom in just a couple of sentences. I internalised that advice almost immediately and, even to this day, live by this principle.

My circle of friends throughout my childhood was terrific. In primary school, we were all curious kids, doing the best we could in the classroom. We'd diligently complete our classes during the day and play innocent games such as tag and 'ice and water', the Malaysian version of 'fire and ice', during recess. We even started a mini business together making and selling friendship bands towards the end of our primary-school years. I found like-minded kids who were hardworking, inquisitive, and studious to call my friends and I loved it.

But when I transitioned to secondary school, things changed. It was almost as soon as I stepped foot into secondary school that it felt like the people I was so accustomed to befriending – the hardworking, diligent ones – became harder to come by.

There were instead a lot of kids who thought smoking was cool, or wearing baggy trousers and untucked shirts was cool. They were disruptive and noisy in the classroom, enjoying the sound of their own voices and cackles as they picked on the kids who went to school to learn – kids like me.

It was during this period that my parents' advice to pick my friends wisely reverberated in my ears. I had to be intentional about choosing my friends in this sea of bad influences, which required effort on my part.

As a twelve- going on thirteen-year-old, peer pressure and the innate desire to be accepted were irresistible temptations. Who doesn't want to be the popular kid in school who has influence over the student cohort? Who doesn't want to be shielded from the vicious attacks that insecure teens subject others to who don't conform? So, to reject the natural flow of entropy required me to say to myself, 'I have to choose my friends wisely because I'll become a reflection of them – if not now, eventually.'

And I believe my decision to pick my friends carefully made all the difference in the trajectory of my life. I made some great friends in high school, a company of friends who eventually meant the difference between my becoming one of the five Malaysian students to be admitted to the University of Oxford in 2007 or a lost soul who smoked and leeched off the people around him.

The saying is true that you morph into the average of the five people you spend the most time with. Surrounding yourself with certain types of people can strongly influence who you become over time. If your closest friends are hardworking and motivated to succeed, like my friends were throughout school, there's a very high chance, it will rub off on to you as well. You'll take on similar habits and mindsets as them when it comes to things such as dreaming big, working hard, and being curious. Your influence will also rub off on them and it creates an evolving environment in a positive direction, each of you reinforcing each other's belief systems and philosophies.

On the other hand, if your close friends are unmotivated or regularly make poor decisions, unfortunately these negative behaviours could start to become normal for you too.

If I wasn't as intentional in picking my friends and ended up hanging out with that wrong clique, the one that partook in underaged smoking, bullying, and classroom disruption, I'd find myself tending toward their negative qualities and there's no chance I'd have made it to Oxbridge. To this day, I'd probably still regret all my early decisions, as I wallowed in my absence of financial independence and an unproductive lifestyle.

Take a look at each person in your innermost social circle. Are you inspired by them? Can you learn positive things from them? Ask yourself, 'Do they elevate my life?' Or do you look at them and feel like they're misguided, still figuring out their own path and, from what you can see, headed down the wrong road. Analyse their behaviours, attitudes, lifestyle habits, and choices and assess whether they're compatible with where you'd like to be.

Your friends should be ambitious and driven to learn continuously and accomplish meaningful personal goals. They shouldn't settle for mediocrity and complacency.

A good litmus test of the right social circle you should be surrounding yourself with is to ask yourself, 'Are my friends planning for the future or are they living aimlessly in the present?' If the latter, they'll hold you back and it's time to cut them out.

The wonderful thing about all of this is that while many things are outside your control in this life, choosing your friends is well within your own control. So, seek out connections with peers who share your core values and ambitious aspirations for growth and progress. Surround yourself with people who'll both challenge and support you to go after that big dream of getting into Oxbridge. Distance yourself from so-called 'friends' if interacting with them no longer fits your vision for the kind of trajectory you want your life to take. Because achieving success, long-term happiness, and your full potential are far too important!

Regularly pull yourself back and evaluate the close friends you choose to spend your time with. Consider carefully how they may be influencing your development and ultimately your ability to achieve your dreams of getting into Oxbridge.

Because getting into the universities of Oxford or Cambridge is an ambitious task. I'm talking about the world's best education institutions here – they accept only a small fraction of applicants each year. Your dream is like a seed to be grown and nurtured, and your circle of friends is the soil, sunlight, and fertiliser you feed it. Being strategic and intentional in building your social network is vital.

Seek out academic clubs, preparatory programmes, and community groups both in and outside school so you can connect with motivated peers. Team activities such as these provide excellent environments for productive interaction with like-minded people who'll support your aspirations.

If possible, build your network with older peers who might already have completed or are in the process of applying to Oxbridge. They can offer valuable mentorship and insights that could take you much longer to learn on your own, thus turbocharging your chances of success. They also give you real-life role models to look up to and ease any doubts you may have about achieving your big dream, because you've seen someone you know achieve what you might have thought was impossible.

As per my parents' wise advice, you're a reflection of the people you surround yourself with – if not now, eventually. So, choose your friends in a purposeful way and start now, just as the Chinese proverb says, 'The best time to plant a tree was 20 years ago. The second best time is now.'

6

Don't care about what other people think of you

Reaching for any ambitious dream requires you to stand out from the crowd. It's in the very definition of 'doing something extraordinary' that you're breaking away from the ordinary and the regular hum of things that most people resign themselves to. And in doing so, you'll expose yourself to people's attention and hence, inevitably their opinions, criticisms, and judgements.

It's only natural. When you dream big dreams and aim high, you must be willing to raise your sights beyond what's normal or average. You'll need to raise your vision and presence above everyone else and work towards heights that others sometimes cannot even see.

When you stick your neck out like this, you'll stand out like a tall tree in the woods. And when you stand out like a tall tree, what happens? You become visible to everyone and suddenly everyone has an opinion of you and what you're doing. Most will likely be good opinions but, by the law of numbers, there will eventually be jealous, resentful, and sometimes even malicious, opinions even if they form just 1 per cent of all opinions. And the taller that giant sequoia grows, the more likely it is to be struck by lightning or become a target for nearby woodcutters.

I experienced this firsthand as a kid who'd set his sights on getting into a top global university.

I was a studious kid and, unlike many others in my high school, I embraced my curiosity for learning and pursued my huge ambitions. This translated into strong competence in the classroom, regular successes in local and regional academic competitions and plenty of scholastic acknowledgements throughout my years of school. And as a fairly rotund, bespectacled boy, I was easy pickings for being bullied as I dared to reach beyond the ordinary.

The bullying got so bad that I'd dread the Mondays after I'd won regional competitions and quizzes. It was customary at my high school to acknowledge students' achievements on the broader stage – whether it was winning a gold medal at the district badminton tournament or being on the podium at the regional chess championships. My school would usually schedule the prize-giving ceremony on the Monday after, during the morning assembly, where our headmistress would present the trophy acquired to the winning student in front of the entire school.

It was supposed to be a proud moment for the champion – one where they were acknowledged and celebrated for bringing honour to the school.

But for me, when I won the district maths quiz or got a gold medal at the Physics Olympiad, I'd dread the Mondays because I'd be met with whistles, cackles, and boos from a small section of the assembled crowd as I gingerly stepped on to the stage to receive the trophies I'd acquired the week before. These were kids from the 'cool gang' who thought it was funny to bully the 'nerd' verbally and emotionally. And, like sheep, many others who probably wanted to be accepted by the 'cool gang' would fortify the gang's noise with their own voices.

My headmistress knew every time she presented me my awards or trophies during the school assembly that I'd be met with raucousness from this unruly group. So much so that she'd mouth the words 'Don't care about them' and offer me a warm comforting smile as I approached her to receive my awards. Her name was Ms Kwan and I'll always remember her kindness.

But what many people don't know is that I'd made a promise to myself at the age of eleven, way before the bullying ever started, not to care about what other people thought of me.

I'm not sure where this deep wisdom came from or how I obtained it but, like my big dreams of getting into a top university, I wrote down on a piece of paper the words 'Don't care what other people think of you' and I've kept it with me ever since – first, as that scrap of paper on my wall but for ever etched in the deepest corners of my mind.

To this day, I don't care about what other people think of me, especially when I'm going after the goals I've set for myself. And I've achieved many successes, from getting into Oxbridge to getting a highly competitive job in the bustling city of London thanks to it.

The decision not to care single-handedly got me through the toughest moments of my high-school years. The bullying was difficult and relentless but I never let it change the course of my ship. I knew what I wanted to achieve and no amount of verbal abuse or social bullying was going to stop me. I would not be bullied into mediocrity!

It isn't easy ignoring the opinions of others, especially as a clueless teenager who's still figuring out life and himself. Being human, we're fundamentally social beings and have evolved over hundreds of thousands of years in tightly knit groups. Our ancestors understood that being accepted and approved by others in their social group was essential for survival. Those who were isolated or outcast faced severe risks, such as the lack of access to resources, protection, and support, especially in times of need.

And so, over generations, we have evolved to crave the acceptance and approval of others. Our brains have developed psychological mechanisms that motivate us to seek acceptance and approval as a means of ensuring safety within our social groups. And hence, when we do get that social acceptance it triggers the brain's pleasure and reward centres. Conversely, facing rejection activates the brain's pain and anxiety centres as a warning of potential threats to our well-being.

It's important to recognise that to do anything significant or important, you won't be able to satisfy everyone. Whether born out of a difference in opinion, because we're all diverse beings, or merely out of jealousy, you'll face opposition from people – especially those who are less advanced in their circumstances than you are. They'll feel the need to make you conform to the norm and conform to mediocrity. Some amount of disagreement and disapproval is inevitable when bucking the status quo to pursue your dreams.

Great pioneers and visionaries throughout history understood this. Nelson Mandela, Mahatma Gandhi, Martin Luther King, Steve Jobs, and many others, all unequivocally knew that satisfying everybody's preference was not compatible with meaningful progress. You'll ruffle feathers when you do anything significant. That's just how it is.

So, while our craving acceptance is genetically hardwired in us, high achievers learn not to let that get in the way of their dreams. They're able to distinguish clearly which group of people's opinions they should value versus which group they should ignore.

It was easy for me to distinguish these groups. I looked at the kinds of people who inspired me, who were role models – these were the people from whom I'd value feedback and guidance. The 'cool gang' at school? They failed to inspire me. I knew long term they would not have the last laugh if I continued to work on myself and my dreams.

Who are your role models? Ask yourself whose opinions you value when it comes to your goals and dreams.

Finally, not caring what other people think of you is also about embracing your authentic self. Achieving ambitious aspirations such as gaining admission to Oxbridge requires it.

The application and selection process inevitably involve putting yourself and your dreams out in the open and you could be met with jealousy from people who wished they could have dreamt as big as you. They'll scrutinise and judge you and it will become easy for you to then second-guess your choices based on how others may perceive them, or anticipating criticism may paralyse you. I could have conformed to the 'cool gang' and abandoned my studies if I succumbed to the social pressure. It would have been easy to do that but I'm grateful that I'd decided early on not to care what other people thought of me as I chased after my dreams of getting into a top university.

Being authentic and overcoming any fear of judgement are core foundational drivers to help you build self-confidence. This allows university admission committees to get a sense of your confident character and understand how you'll enrich their student community and the broader institution. Being fuelled by authenticity and self-confidence, rather than by the need to please perceived expectations, empowers a compelling personal statement, and allows you to express your true self during the interviews, which will set you up for success during the Oxbridge application process.

So, remember, 'Don't care what other people think of you.' Dream big, go after your dreams, and never let anyone pressure you into mediocrity!

7

Discipline, discipline, discipline

Getting into an elite university such as Oxford or Cambridge requires an immense amount of effort, focus and, very importantly, *discipline*. However, the discipline I'm referring to is not one that's imposed upon you by other people or external sources. It's not from complying to your parents' wishes or your teachers' and tutors' expectations. It's self-discipline – the kind where you're accountable to yourself and the things you say you'll do in order to achieve the lofty goals you've set for yourself. It's the intrinsic ability to stick to your goals and commitments without someone else motivating you.

This means having the restraint to say no to temptations that could distract you from productive activities, even when no one is watching you. It means diligently following the routines, plans, and schedules you've set for yourself every day in the effort of bettering your skills and strengthening your case for being accepted into Oxbridge, whether that be in the quality of your grades or the depth of your extracurricular experiences.

As a teen, I was intentional about building my self-discipline. I always created a plan and schedule when embarking on any endeavour and always followed it. No excuses.

When it came to my studies, I built a routine where I'd spend one to two hours every evening revising the materials I'd learnt that day at school. I'd not allow myself to be tempted by the new video game I'd purchased for my Sega console over the weekend (for that, I'd given myself two hours over the weekends to enjoy). So long as it was eight in the evening on a Monday through to Friday, I was burying my nose in the vast amounts of academic literature and materials I'd been taught, in order to reinforce the knowledge I'd gained – from Archimedes' principle of displacement to the history of Malaysia's road to independence.

And as far as exams were concerned, I always started revising for them three months in advance, sometimes even six for the most important ones. Occasionally, I'd choose to skip some of my (less close) friends' birthday parties and limit my time at dinners with extended family to ensure I was hitting the specific milestones I'd set out for myself in my revision plans. If I said I'd finish revising chapters 7 to 9 by the week before the exam, I'd 100 per cent do it.

This high level of accountability and self-discipline extended to every facet of my life. I never missed a single taekwondo lesson even though I didn't have a passion for martial arts. Come eight in the morning every Saturday, I'd be present and committed in my freshly pressed white uniform. Rain or shine, I was there.

When I decided at age twelve that I didn't want to be known as 'the fatty' in my school, I set out a plan to lose the weight in six months, adopting a high fibre, low carb diet and running three kilometres twice a day. If you're even remotely familiar with the Asian culture and, in particular, the Malaysian culture, you'll know how important food is in everything we do. It's at the very core of how we connect with each other and there's a popular saying in Malaysia that 'we don't eat to live; we live to eat'. And so, the pressure to break my diet would be incessant, from my parents, relatives, friends, and everyone around me. But I never broke. And, as for the running, I never skipped once. And guess what? I lost all the weight in two-and-a-half months, not six. I was so disciplined I was elected as 'Head of Discipline' twice when I served on the board of prefects in high school!

Now, you may read this and think, 'OK, maybe Julian is just built differently.'

I have to tell you I wasn't always like this. Building this level of self-discipline was no easy task. It required gradually developing habits over several months and years that soon became second nature to me.

It started by my dedicating a couple of hours each evening to revising my subjects, and then adding a new routine by starting my day with a short, slow-paced jog around my neighbourhood. From that, the commitment to stick to what I said I'd do, started to permeate everything I did, from Saturday taekwondo lessons to sticking to my revision schedules. Before long, I'd built this muscle to adhere to my routines with steely resolve and consistency.

The hardest part of building self-discipline is not the effort itself in developing routines and sticking to them – it's making the decision that you'll commit yourself to your goals and, in doing so, exercise self-restraint and discipline. Once I made that decision, execution was intuitive and straightforward.

Having said all this, while having self-discipline to stick to plans is important for success, I want also to clarify that this doesn't preclude having the flexibility that's crucial for adapting to change.

Especially in this day and age where change continues to happen at an unprecedented rate, maintaining flexibility in mindset and approach is crucial.

Developing strong self-discipline through structures such as routines and schedules ensures progress is made towards objectives on a consistent basis. However, no plan or goal is meant to be followed rigidly if circumstances shift drastically. As I committed myself to the plans and routines I set out, I also regularly evaluated their effectiveness and tweaked the course I was taking if needed.

Getting into Oxbridge requires building grit and resilience through hard work and self-restraint. Create a routine for yourself and stick to it (so long as it remains relevant to your goals) to reinforce your self-discipline.

In my own journey of building self-discipline, there were two very valuable rules I learnt about and took to heart, which helped me tremendously.

First, the '21-day rule'. Originating from a book called *Psycho-Cybernetics* by Maxwell Maltz, this rule says that it takes twenty-one days to form a new habit or for a new behaviour to become automatic.

When I wanted to build a new habit or break an old one, I stuck with it consistently for at least twenty-one days. Repeating an action each day for three weeks felt long enough for me to rewire my brain. I didn't miss a day in this twenty-one-day window. Even if it meant having to truncate the action or do an 80 per cent version of it because of time constraints, I'd still follow through. The twenty-one-day rule helped me so much that I started to place increased importance in the number 21. This is not backed by science, but I also found that if I needed to memorise facts such as the capitals of countries around the world or the sequence of chemical elements on the periodic table, repeating them twenty-one times to myself during my revisions was a winning strategy.

The second rule is the '2-day rule', which says never miss two days in a row when you're working towards something.

According to a study published in the *European Journal of Social Psychology*, researchers found that missing a single day of a particular habit has close to zero impact on your long-term ability to stick to that habit. We're all human – we slip up sometimes and this is OK so long as you find a way to get back on track. But if you skip the action for two days in a row, it becomes much easier to keep putting it off and break the routine you're trying to form.

One mistake could be put down as an anomaly, but two mistakes start a pattern.

So, after the initial twenty-one-day window where I'd strictly follow the '21-day rule', I'd continue with this '2-day rule' to help keep me accountable and solidify my routine. Following these two rules helped me significantly when I worked to build strong self-discipline and positive habits, and I believe they can help you too.

Sometimes it can feel like the immediate rewards of showing restraint and exercising self-discipline are so far away and intangible that it becomes demotivating, especially when social pressures feel irresistible. But it's this muscle you strengthen that will ultimately pay off.

Delaying gratification will play a big part in your success. Studies have shown that the ability to delay gratification during formative years in childhood is associated with improved academic performance and greater social competence down the line – two vital ingredients if you want to get into a top university such as Oxford or Cambridge.

The strength, commitment, and work ethic you cultivate through building good habits and self-discipline set strong foundations not only for gaining a place at one of the world's most prestigious universities, but will help you thrive once you're there and under its rigorous academic demands.

Self-discipline is the vital skill that will help you through to the finish line!

8

Work hard to increase your luck

I'm a big believer in luck and the role it plays in every success story you've ever read or heard.

Take the discovery of penicillin for example. In 1928, Alexander Fleming returned from his holiday to find a kind of mould growing in his petri dish of staphylococcus bacteria that prevented the bacteria from growing around it. This led to the discovery of penicillin and subsequently the invention of antibiotics, which have saved millions of lives. Or look more recently at J.K. Rowling, one of the world's most successful authors and the creator of the adored Harry Potter series. She found it difficult to get her manuscript in front of publishers, but one lucky day her stories of the bespectacled wizard made it out of the slush pile because a publisher's child happened to read and love her story.

History is littered with examples of success stories unlocked by luck. Larry Page and Sergey Brin, the founders of Google benefited from being at the right place at the right time when they launched their search engine, as the internet was on its upwards trajectory. Walt Disney struggled for years, but a breakthrough came when he one day serendipitously collaborated with Ub

Iwerks to co-create the beloved Mickey Mouse, who then paved the way for the entertainment mega empire that we see today. Or just look at basketball legend Michael Jordan, one of the most decorated basketball players of all time. You could argue that his being dropped from his high-school basketball team was a lucky turning point for him, because it fed his insatiable hunger for improvement to stratospheric heights, ultimately cementing him as one of the greats of the sport.

Scientists from the University of Catania conducted a study on the role of luck in success and failure and concluded that the most successful individuals are the luckiest ones, and the least successful individuals are the unluckiest ones.

But why do successful people tend to be luckier than the average person?

There's an old saying that 'luck is when preparation meets opportunity'. On the surface, luck seems entirely random – we attribute positive outcomes to being in the right place at the right time through no effort of our own. But upon deeper reflection, I've come to believe that one of the most powerful drivers of luck is something completely within our control and that's hard work. Simply sweating it out, pushing past tiredness, and giving your all.

It's almost as if you can manipulate the amount of luck you experience in your life by adjusting how much effort and hard work you put in.

While randomness and chance play a role, it seems our ability to recognise and take advantage of opportunities is amplified through diligence, effort, and perseverance. Those who work hard are constantly putting themselves in a position to benefit from luck. They expand their skills, knowledge, and network so that when serendipity strikes, they're prepared to seize the moment.

They're also constantly trying their hardest and never giving up, which helps to put them in front of a never-ending corridor of opportunities, so that by the sheer law of numbers they're bound to hit the jackpot at some point. Meanwhile, being passive, lazy, and unprepared means the number of opportunities shrink dramatically and any lucky break goes unexploited.

Look at the examples of the successful people I've mentioned – Alexander Fleming, J.K. Rowling, Larry Page, Sergey Brin, Walt Disney, and Michael Jordan. They all benefited from luck no doubt, but were or are all workaholics who left little to chance.

How many petri dishes did Alexander Fleming test on before he discovered penicillin? How many manuscripts, iterations, and rejections did J.K. Rowling have to work through before Harry Potter was published? How many late nights did Larry and Sergey have to pull in coding and setting up Google? I don't know the exact numbers to each of these questions but I can assure you that the answer to all of them is, 'A lot!'

Behind every 'lucky' break is usually a long, arduous trail of sweat and dedication that paved the way. Their perseverance and hard work expanded the scope of possibilities so more opportunities could open to them – remember our world is governed by the law of numbers! Hard work also builds confidence and competence, so they were able to capitalise effectively on opportunities that came up and spot chances others would have missed.

Hard work manipulates luck in our favour. By expending copious time and energy working towards our goals, we tilt the odds in our favour to experience more good fortune in our pursuits.

Getting into an elite institution such as Oxford or Cambridge certainly requires an element of luck – there's no doubt about it. The competition is intense, with only a small fraction of highly qualified and talented students gaining admission each year.

However, like the success stories of Alexander Fleming, J.K. Rowling and Walt Disney, hard work can give us control over the frequency of luck in our lives and, more specifically, in our university applications. It's very much within our power to attract fortunate happenstance through hard work and increase the chances of achieving what may seem like an out-of-reach dream. Those who put in extensive preparation embarking on their Oxbridge journey are far more likely to find themselves in the right place at the right time to receive an acceptance letter from their dream university.

Speaking from personal experience, I can confidently say that my own ability to dig deep and work hard towards my goals showed me a powerful way of magnetizing positive opportunities. All the scholarships I was so lucky to receive that helped pay for my education (from A-levels to my undergraduate course at the University of Oxford, to my PhD programme at the University of Cambridge) were the result of staying up that extra hour to solidify my understanding of quadratic, polynomial and logarithmic functions. They were the result of taking up the presidential position in my school's English society even though I was already serving in three other leadership positions in clubs and societies after school. They were the result of putting my hand up and saying yes to representing my school in the upcoming district championships for physics even if I was already stretched a lot, juggling schoolwork, extracurricular activities, and creative hobbies.

Having a solid work ethic is a prerequisite for being admitted to Oxbridge, and doing anything successful in life for that matter. Don't be afraid of hard work. Embrace it, have discipline, show initiative, be reliable, and take pride in your efforts. Stay motivated to push yourself to create more lucky opportunities for success, which will turn you from a 'maybe' case to a 'must admit' case when Oxbridge or any top university evaluates your profile.

And once admitted, you'll find that the strong work ethic you cultivated over the years in preparation for applying to Oxbridge, will be one of the most important ingredients for your own success during your time pursuing your degree.

Depending on the course, the admission rates for undergraduate courses at Oxbridge could be as low as 4 per cent. That is, for every twenty-five applicants, twenty-four of them are unsuccessful. Working hard increases your luck so you're fortunate enough to be the one who gets in. Always give your teachers your full attention in classes. Work hard to complete every piece of homework you've been assigned. Take up leadership positions in clubs and societies. Volunteer your time and energy to help charities and your community. Intern at companies and always give it your all.

Passionate students work hard to expand their skill sets and perspectives, impressing university admission committees with both the qualifications and confidence needed to excel if given the opportunity. They make it impossible for luck not to intersect with their ambition at some point.

Remember that in this world you can make your own luck, and working hard stacks the odds in your favour. So, go out there, sweat it out, push past tiredness and give it your all!

As Samuel Goldwyn, the American film producer once said, 'The harder I work, the luckier I get!'

9
Focus on learning

It's just past noon on one of my most important Saturdays ever. I extend my hand to give a firm handshake to a bearded man with kind eyes by the name of Dr Peter McFadden. Dr McFadden or 'Peter', as he preferred to be called, was my Oxford interviewer (and eventual tutor as well) and we had just concluded forty-five rigorous minutes exploring the laws of physics through billiard balls, internal combustion engines, and complex equations. In the lush halls of a five-star hotel in Kuala Lumpur, he shakes my hand and says, 'Your passion for learning is evident. It was great to spend the time with you.'

'Your passion for learning is evident' – those words still reverberate through my ears. They validated my approach to life and reinforced my belief that being teachable and having a learning mindset were going to be key to my academic success.

And, true enough, a few weeks later, I received that coveted email confirming I'd become a University of Oxford student the next year, fulfilling my biggest dream as a young man.

I've always focused on learning. I believe that learning about the world around us is one of the greatest gifts life can offer us. From a young age, I found joy in discovering new things, asking questions, and expanding my mind with knowledge. The more I learnt, the more acutely aware I became of the fact that what I know must be infinitesimally small relative to all that's left for me to discover. But plugging those gaps with novel ideas and connections brought me profound fulfilment. I loved learning because each new idea or insight felt like a new adventure.

And while many people learn because they want to please their parents or to pass their next test, I think at some basic level it's important to learn for learning's sake. This means to learn because you're genuinely interested in knowing. It means bathing in your curiosity in a way that can sometimes feel self-indulgent. It means finding joy in discovery and exploration.

What I know for sure is that my lifelong focus on learning is a key reason I've achieved many of my goals. Getting into Oxbridge was certainly a dream come true, but if I took the time to reflect thoroughly on these achievements, I'd argue that they were just milestones among many in my ongoing journey for learning. My excellent academic track record was less a result of competitive motivation than of approaching each of my subjects with curiosity and wanting to understand them for understanding's sake.

So, while getting into a top university was always a goal of mine, my primary motivation at a visceral level transcended that. I found energy in focusing on the true reason for wanting to get an elite education. And in having that focus on learning, I also found peace whatever the outcome of my university application would be, because the university was a means to an end and not the end itself. The end was always to build upon learning and continually deepen my understanding of the world. This allowed me to relax into the process and helped me perform when it mattered, instead of being stressed out to the detriment of my own chances of getting admitted.

Having a learning mindset also crucially means having a mindset for continuous improvement. Being focused on learning is about cultivating a spirit of perpetual progress because you recognise that you don't know everything and there's always more to learn, always more you can improve on. It's about aiming to be 1 per cent or even just 0.1 per cent better at the end of every day because you've cultivated the humility and enthusiasm for growth.

Atomic Habits by James Clear, arguably one of the most popular self-help books of all time, compellingly explains that progress is made by small, consistent improvements over long periods of time. If you aim to get 1 per cent better every day, you may not notice the change by the end of each day, but by the end of the year you'll end up being thirty-seven times better than when you started.

Adopting a learning mindset is about embracing this principle at the core of your approach to life. You go to bed each night asking yourself, 'What have I learnt today that has made me a 1 per cent better version of myself than at the start of the day?'

I regularly ended my days reflecting on this question. I'd find answers in everything – that white light consists of seven colours, that the First World War ended on 11 November 1918, that force is equal to mass times acceleration, that nobody can hurt you without your permission. Insights that I realised would stay with me for ever, which I never had in my prior life – a pretty cool thought!

These sessions of reflection brought me immense joy, especially during long and difficult days. They reminded me that I was continuing to upskill myself, however small the steps were, by being a student not just in the classroom but a student of the world more broadly. I was harnessing my mental energy towards small improvements within my control, knowing that I was and never would be a finished product, but was always becoming a better version to the benefit of myself and the people around me.

So, on days when there weren't major achievements to give me a confidence boost or on days where failure would rear its ugly head, I'd always be reminded that my focus on learning had driven growth regardless. Steady, inevitable growth that will one day compound to becoming transformational. And it did become transformational.

The wonder of learning is that the more you focus on it, the better you become at it. You sharpen your ability to learn fast!

The ability to learn fast is an incredibly valuable skill. In today's fast-paced world where change is the only constant, our ability to absorb and process new information rapidly is crucial for success. This is especially true for achieving academic success and getting into a prestigious university such as Oxford or Cambridge.

The rigorous academic programmes at Oxbridge demand that students be able to grasp complex concepts, theories, and large amounts of content at an accelerated pace. Being able to learn quickly and efficiently will allow you to cover more material in less time, ensuring you're better prepared for any assessment or examination. It frees up time for you to go after more goals so that you're able to supplement your excellent academic results with equally strong extracurricular achievements.

I hope it's clear by now that your focus for learning should extend beyond just your studies. It should be part of your culture and your habits, permeating every aspect of your life. It should also be about learning by observing others – the positive traits to emulate as well as mistakes to avoid. Identifying role models whose character and accomplishments are worth mimicking. This was something I did a lot growing up. I watched my role models closely and learnt, for example, eloquence, kindness, and gravitas from my ultimate role model Oprah Winfrey, never skipping an episode of her talk show, which aired every weekday afternoon when I was a teenager.

Finally, having a learning mindset will allow you never to be afraid of not knowing. This bold courage when stepping into the unknown is one of the most powerful skills you can have in life. You become unafraid because not only do you already have the humility to accept that you can't know everything, but you also have the confidence to be able to ask the right questions to eventually be enlightened.

For me, my focus on learning meant that I was unafraid to look 'stupid' in the classroom by putting up my hand to ask my teachers questions around concepts I was unclear about. I learnt how to ask the right questions to get the clarity I needed and I learnt to be resourceful when I didn't always get the answers I was looking for.

Ultimately, developing a mindset of continuous, passionate learning should be the goal for anyone aspiring to get into highly selective universities such as Oxbridge. While strong academic results will be a primary barometer for your university admission, it's your demonstrated enthusiasm and focus for learning that will enable your entry and differentiate you from the pack.

Focus on finding joy in learning, continuous improvement, learning fast, being a student in and out of the classroom, and asking good questions. You'll find that the coveted opportunities you seek will follow naturally. But, more importantly, you'll thrive regardless of any situation, and getting into Oxbridge will seem like a natural step in your own journey.

10

It's not where you are but where you're going

Most of us will be familiar with workout music, the kind you blast into your eardrums as you power through that last mile on your treadmill or push through those final few dumbbell presses. You know, the songs that give you strength to push yourself that little bit further, when it feels like you're about to succumb to the fatigue and pain.

My workout playlist is extensive but right at the top is a song by a band called The Hours titled 'Ali in the Jungle'. It goes:

It's not how you start; it's how you finish,
And it's not where you're from; it's where you're at.
Everybody gets knocked down,
Everybody gets knocked down,
How quick are you gonna get up?
How quick are you gonna get up?

And then there's my favourite verse that goes:

It's not where you are; it's where you're going,

Where are you going?

And it's not about the things you've done; it's what you're doing now.

What are you doing now?

I absolutely love this song because it encapsulates one of my central philosophies in life from which I derive limitless energy and motivation – to not focus on whatever your circumstance may be, but to focus on where you're going.

The profound implications of this philosophy are twofold. First, it speaks to the realisation that your current circumstance is not the determinant of your final destination. This is potent because it places the power to exert change right back into your own hands. You realise you're not a victim of your own predicament and wherever your starting point in life may be – you're in full control of how you reach where you want to be. Second, but more importantly for me, is that your focus shifts away from things outside your control – principally, what's happened in your past or what you anticipate in your future – so that you're living fully in the present and are controlling what you can control as part of your journey to achieving your dreams.

I've always lived by this philosophy: to *focus on the journey and where I'm going* above everything else. And it was only until a few years later that I discovered 'Ali in the Jungle' by The Hours, by chance, watching one of the most inspiring commercials I'd ever seen (by Nike of course), where the tune served as a backing track to a montage of top athletes pushing themselves to greatness, getting up when being knocked down, and living by Nike's famous slogan 'Just Do It'. I'd highly recommend you search 'Nike commercial – human chain, Ali in the Jungle' on YouTube or Google. It's an inspiring one-minute masterpiece of a video.

I tell you all this because getting into Oxbridge is no mean feat. You'll get knocked down and it's natural to be filled with doubts as you set your sights on it. These doubts could stem from your current circumstances – that perhaps you think you're not good enough, not smart enough, not rich enough or not brave enough. Maybe doubts stem from your vision of the future – that perhaps you'll fail, that no university will want to accept you or that you won't thrive even if accepted.

The allure of an elite university can lead hopeful applicants to lose sight of the present. This chapter articulates why focusing on the journey is key to a successful Oxbridge application. Aspiring

Oxbridge applicants will serve themselves well by focusing on enjoying the journey over the destination of securing a place.

Enjoying the journey means finding joy in being fully immersed, present, and engaged in each step of the preparation, whether it's poring over your textbooks and revision materials ahead of your mid-term exams, giving your all at your extracurricular activities in the early mornings of a weekend, or reflecting deeply on what subjects you'd like to pursue at university when the time comes. Valuing the process and gaining satisfaction in the pursuit itself, as opposed to viewing it as merely a means to achieving a goal is so important.

First, it allows you to perform at your best when it matters most. Being fully present and immersed as part of your path to Oxbridge allows you to dedicate all your energy, attention, and focus to the task at hand, whether it's the foundational work you need to do a few years before you even submit your application or it's the compelling personal statement and upcoming interview you're preparing for. You'll find that by not being distracted by the past or the future and just being focused on the present, the quality of your effort elevates significantly.

You no longer become caught up in dreaming and worrying about hypothetical futures, such as whether you'll receive an offer or not, which helps keep your anxiety levels in check. You regain a sense of control over all aspects you have influence over in the present and you'll be able to execute what you need to execute excellently with this focus, and ultimately be rewarded for it.

Second, your journey to Oxbridge is fundamentally about your own personal growth, not just the boost to your CV (or ego) that getting into a top university could give you.

Striving each day to learn something new and, through that, strengthening your application is a much more effective approach than placing all your attention on the destination of getting into Oxbridge alone. If the emphasis is tilted too heavily on the outcome of securing a place, you risk missing out on the valuable lessons, experiences, and skill sets obtained along the way.

This is not only to the detriment of your overall application, but will be to the detriment of your future self as well. It's important to realise that each step of your journey builds skills, knowledge, relationships, and habits that contribute to your overall growth, development, and success.

The mistakes you make and setbacks you experience along the way provide learning opportunities that help to build resilience and improve your outlook. A narrow focus on the destination misses these chances to learn and become better. Remaining present allows the inherent rewards of exploring the challenging path to Oxbridge to be fully realised as you walk it. And you can ultimately approach the process with reduced stress and greater productivity.

Third, you'll be happier because your happiness is not contingent on the outcome of gaining entry to Oxbridge. You'll learn to derive your joy from the journey itself – from growing as a person through new experiences, challenging yourself, discovering your passions, and becoming comfortable with uncertainty. Ultimately, finding a level of purpose as part of your journey to Oxbridge will bring contentment. And focusing on the big picture of this will ensure your happiness, regardless of the outcome. Nothing is more important than that.

Your motivation can also be significantly enhanced by being present and focusing on the journey. You begin to notice the small wins and progress you're making along the way and can start to build momentum through these tiny victories.

Remember that life is a series of small steps and you build momentum through every positive development no matter how small it may be. Celebrate your progress often, through reviewing your daily goals and plans as part of your journey to Oxbridge. You'll find that maintaining your drive is much easier because you're able to build an ongoing sense of achievement.

Finally, it's important to focus on the journey more than the destination because life is unpredictable and being flexible to opportunities will ensure you're constantly able to adapt and optimise for your situation. Your journey may lead to altered goals as you learn more about yourself, the process, and the destination as well. It's important to remain open to unexpected lessons or opportunities that may emerge. Being too fixated on the destination risks your missing out on this. The reality is that you cannot anticipate everything and your journey can lead to new destinations as your understanding deepens. Being attuned to the journey itself will ensure you make the right decisions for yourself every step of the way.

As the great Ralph Waldo Emerson once said, 'Life is a journey, not a destination.'

As enticing as the rewards of Oxbridge may seem, if you're not enjoying the long path as you prepare for them, you probably won't enjoy the experience when you get there.

Therefore, focus on what's most important – the journey you're making to realising your Oxbridge dreams, and you'll reap the rewards you're aiming for as a by-product of your efforts, as counterintuitive as that may seem!

11

Be positive

I've always had a love of music. It was instilled in me by my dad, who would blast the stereo with his favourite tunes at any and all times of the day. When I was around ten or eleven, I remember walking into the living room to 'The Best' by Tina Turner put on blast, exactly at the moment when my dad turned around and pointed at me, singing, 'You're simply the best, better than all the rest, better than anyone, anyone I've ever met!'

Many years later I made the connection that the song was originally a love song, but its association for me has always been about being your best, being better than the competition, and never doubting yourself. It was about the power of having a positive mindset, something my father never let my brother and I forget growing up.

One of his favourite phrases that he used to drill into us was, 'There's no such thing as "cannot".' It sometimes got annoying growing up hearing those words whenever things got tricky for us, but my dad obliterated the concept of 'impossible' by showing us the sheer power of being positive. And it's because of this that I ultimately had the audacity to dream as big as I did, setting my sights on an elite university education, which, let's be honest, would have seemed impossible without this mindset.

The road to Oxbridge is long and arduous. Any of us who aspires to study there knows that we'll need top A-level grades as well as an intensely well-rounded application showcasing our passions, leadership skills, and community involvement. It's a process that can seem overwhelming and impossible at times. Being positive and believing in yourself is crucial if you're to succeed in the face of the many setbacks and rejections you're sure to experience along the way.

This brazen belief that you have what it takes to join the ranks of esteemed Oxbridge alumni, the likes of J.R.R. Tolkien, Tim Berners-Lee, Stephen Hawking, and even Isaac Newton, stems from having an unshakeable positive attitude and belief in your own abilities when you're still discovering yourself and the world around you. You need this brazen belief if you're to seize the opportunities in front of you.

The benefits of staying positive are boundless. One of the greatest advantages is you develop a solution-oriented mindset. By maintaining a positive outlook, you no longer see challenges as mere problems, but as opportunities. Your focus shifts from dwelling on what's difficult, to what you can do to solve the issue. Suddenly, you become more resourceful and make a habit of finding solutions instead of lamenting problems.

Positive thinking has been shown to improve problem-solving skills. A 2018 study conducted by researchers at the Stanford University School of Medicine found that in children aged seven to ten, being positive improved their ability to answer mathematics problems, increased their memories, and enhanced their problem-solving skills. Through magnetic resonance imaging (MRI) brain scans, they found that being positive physiologically boosted the functions of the hippocampus, the part of the brain responsible for memory, and constructively influenced learning.

This shouldn't be too surprising – a positive mindset forces you to stay focused on potential answers and resolutions rather than what's already failed. You don't waste your time complaining about your setbacks, but instead channel that energy into looking at the positives, reviewing what you've learnt and building from there. You're less likely to feel helpless, because you believe that every problem is solvable. And, over time, this solution-seeking approach becomes a tremendously useful life skill, empowering your own resourcefulness in realising solutions. This will give you a winning advantage in tackling challenging problems on your journey to Oxbridge, whether it's the mind-bending brainteasers you're asked during your interview, the scientific concept you couldn't quite grasp in the morning lecture, or something else entirely.

Maintaining a positive outlook is also a highly effective way to boost motivation and drive – crucial ingredients to achieving success in any context. Being positive means focusing on what's going well. And when you focus on your successes, no matter how small they may be, it builds confidence and reinforces your belief in yourself. You invite gratitude into your life and, before long, you start to feel more determined and empowered in your ability to achieve your dreams, which spurs you on to working harder to make your Oxbridge goals a reality.

This was certainly true for me. If you asked me what the positive things were that I'd achieved on my journey to Oxford and Cambridge that built the foundations of my success there, I could share with you an unending list of achievements – winning the state physics quiz, captaining my school's squash team at the state championships, scoring straight A's at the Malaysian equivalent of the O-level exams, being top of my class for most of my high school and college years . . . The list goes on. But if you asked me what my setbacks were, my initial instinct would be to think, 'Why dwell on them?' or 'They weren't failures: they were foundations to my future successes.'

If I really wanted to look at the negatives, I could. For example, I captained my school's squash team but we lost in the semi-finals of the state championship. Or I scored straight A's in my O-levels but they were nine A1s and one A2, with that A2 ruining what could have been a perfect record. But I never let myself perceive things that way. It was neither productive nor constructive to my broader ambitions, and my focus on the things that were going well gave me huge amounts of motivation, energy, and drive. I knew that wherever I was, I was not a finished product and every achievement or setback played a crucial part in my journey to getting into Oxbridge. This in turn helped me become a better version of myself on good days and helped me weather the difficult bad days. It really comes down to how you frame the outlook on your life.

You'll find that your stress and anxiety levels will plummet when you adopt a positive mindset, allowing you to think more clearly during your classes and, crucially, your examinations. It's easier to perform your best when you're in a calm state of mind.

Conversely, if you have a negative mindset, you'll criticise yourself when things go wrong, which will not only add stress but also lower your self-esteem and confidence. This could then create a negative spiral undoing all the progress you've made.

Use positivity to increase your resilience in the face of failure or rejection. Oxbridge looks for persistence and determination as much as academic abilities, so this simple decision to choose positivity will show that you have what it takes to be successful in Oxford or Cambridge.

Lift up the people around you with your positivity. Learn to project genuine, good vibes. It rubs off on others, makes you more likable and helps you make a good impression. You'll connect better with your Oxbridge interviewer as well, who's likelier to feel a good connection with a prospective student who exudes positivity, confidence, and enthusiasm than one who doesn't. Also, you'll be able to connect better with your teachers and tutors, who'll then want to support you and your dreams more.

These are a few tips and tricks I've used throughout my life to maintain my positive attitude:

- I celebrate my small wins, no matter how small.

- Before I go to bed, I reflect on three things I'm grateful for that have happened throughout the day.

- I regularly repeat affirmations to myself, whether from notes I've written to myself or when I'm in front of the mirror, such as 'You can do it.' Or sometimes even, 'There's no such thing as "cannot"!' (My dad would be proud of this.)

- I try to limit my usage of social media to three times a day and don't look at my phone in the first twenty minutes after I wake up. When growing up, we had no social media or mobile phones, so I adopted this only post-Oxbridge – life used to be much simpler!

- I do hard exercise at least twice a week and maintain a baseline routine of light exercise for six days of the week.

- I make sure to get seven to eight hours of sleep every night.

- And, most importantly, I surround myself with positive people (and cut negative people out of my life).

These small, consistent practices help me maintain my positivity levels and I hope they'll be helpful to you too.

To emphasise again, getting into Oxbridge requires copious amounts of positivity, motivation, and perseverance. Without these, the journey will be unmanageable and the goal out of reach.

12
Stay humble and hungry

Once you start putting into practice the lessons of the previous chapters, I guarantee you'll start seeing a marked improvement in your outlook on Oxbridge. Your grades will start to ascend, you'll start topping your class in certain subjects and, before long, you'll top your year on aggregate. Your extracurricular activities and achievements will pile up, and you'll have a great network of people cheering you on, supporting you, and providing you access to opportunities that will help in your Oxbridge application. You'll rise in this virtuous cycle and experience what they call 'purple patches' – exceptional periods where you'll be on a run of success and good luck. You'll feel unstoppable.

In these moments, it can become exceedingly easy to allow contentment, overconfidence, and entitlement to creep in. Why not? Things are going well. You feel in complete control of your destiny and opportunities start to feel within reach. And then, the contentment you start feeling leads to complacency, your overconfidence blinds you to your areas for improvement, and your growing sense of entitlement erodes your work ethic and introduces negativity into your psyche.

I've always believed that as sweet as success is, success is also the worst teacher. It's important always to remind yourself to stay humble and hungry.

To stay humble means staying grounded, maintaining a modest attitude, and showing gratitude in the captivating aura of success. It's about recognising your strengths and accomplishments without developing a sense of superiority or entitlement, acknowledging that there's always so much more you can learn and that you're far from a finished product. You recognise and appreciate the contributions of others in your success, seek feedback and advice to improve, and remain open-minded to new ideas and perspectives.

Staying hungry, on the other hand, is about maintaining your strong drive and ambition for continuous growth and improvement regardless of the level of success you're experiencing. It's this feeling of always striving for more, the relentless desire to continue pushing boundaries, setting new goals, and constantly challenging yourself. It means not settling for mediocrity or becoming complacent with your achievements. It's about maintaining your passion for your work, your thirst for knowledge, and your commitment to ongoing self-improvement.

This combination of staying humble and staying hungry is incredibly powerful. It forms the foundation of a strong, growth-oriented mindset and helped me avoid stagnancy and complacency in my long journey to achieving my dreams of getting an elite university education.

As they say in sports, the game is not over until the final whistle blows. You may be 5–0 up in a football match with just ten minutes remaining on the clock, but anything can happen during those ten minutes. You need to stay focused, not get ahead of yourself, and continue to push. Widen that lead and never take your opponent for granted.

You may be on track for a successful Oxbridge application. You may have finished your high school at the top of your year, are on track for straight A's in your A-level exams, and secured tremendous references from the best teachers and mentors. But, until you step foot into the hallowed halls of your Oxford or Cambridge college, the proverbial whistle has not yet blown. Your personal statement may not be as good as it needs to be, or you could be stumped by a brainteaser given by your interviewer, or you could fail to achieve the required grades set out in your university offer. (Note: It's standard practice for universities in the UK to offer a place to a prospective student on the condition that they meet certain grades for their final A-level results. For me, this was three A's to secure my place at Oxford University. If you fail to achieve the grades stipulated, you forfeit your offer of admission to the university.)

This is why it's so important to stay humble and hungry in the face of triumph and success.

Prolific poet Rudyard Kipling said it best in his poem 'If': 'If you can meet with Triumph and Disaster, and treat those two impostors just the same . . .'

You must not only exercise restraint in the face of disaster and failure, not letting your disappointment get in the way of future endeavours, but also treat triumph and success the same – exercise restraint, not letting your ego get in the way of further improvement.

Recognise that there's always more to learn, even more so when you're on a purple patch because you have the momentum built from your previous triumphs to provide powerful winds that can propel you higher – but only if your sails remain open to new learning and ways of improvement.

To remain productive, you must understand that no matter how much progress has been made, the potential for further progress remains. Continue being teachable. Stay open and seek feedback, new ideas, and alternative views.

Remember that we stand on the shoulders of the giants before us. Our successes are not achieved purely by our own volition or effort. The support from our family and loved ones from emotional to financial, the patience from our teachers and mentors who share their knowledge and expertise, the encouragement and positivity from our friends, colleagues, and people we choose to surround ourselves with, have all played an important role in helping us achieve our dreams.

Show gratitude towards the privilege you have. Stay other-oriented and show appreciation to everyone whose paths have crossed yours.

Even those who haven't been supportive, such as the bullies you've had to endure – appreciate them because they gave you clarity and strength to press forward in your pursuit of your dreams. Staying humble in this way will foster stronger relationships and mentorships that will ultimately come back to serve you. It's that simple thing called karma.

Staying humble and hungry is about giving everything you've got and expecting nothing in return. You give your all and strive for more but, at the same time, you're grateful for what you have. There's an interesting tension between being humble and hungry – they pose an interesting contradiction. Unlocking the ability to execute each to its highest degree will ensure happiness and success are achieved in a way where neither is contingent on the other.

Growing up, a key morsel of wisdom I kept with me, also scribbled on a piece of paper, were the four words 'Give everything, expect nothing'.

These four words helped me realign my focus whenever I felt that things were going exceedingly badly or exceedingly well. The core of this wisdom is finding motivation and drive as well as your satisfaction and fulfilment in life from sources other than your successes or achievements.

For me, while the dream was always to get into an elite university, I never expected I would. I nonetheless gave it my all, leaving nothing on the table. And when I finally received that momentous email from Oxford University confirming my acceptance, I experienced one of the most intensely joyous moments of my life grounded in pure gratitude and humility, because I never expected it. I believe it's because I took this approach that I was ultimately rewarded for it.

The final thing I'll leave you with to contemplate is, 'Run your own race.'

If you're like me, staying hungry runs freely in your blood. I'm naturally a very competitive person. I want to be the best in every endeavour I set out to do. Top of class, top of my year, sports captain, president of multiple societies . . . Play a board game with me, and you'll stare into the face of someone determined to win.

It took me many years to learn that winning isn't about beating the competition – it's about beating your own standards that you've set for yourself. The race you run in life is your own. True competition is only with yourself.

So, as you set your sights on Oxbridge, or any top university for that matter, remember to run your own race. Don't compare yourself with others – it will only breed envy and anxiety. Focus on yourself, focus on what you can control in the moment.

Echoing the sage words of filmmaker Baz Luhrmann, 'Sometimes you're ahead, sometimes you're behind, the race is long, and in the end, it's only with yourself.'

Part 2

The Process

With the foundation laid in the previous chapters, it's now down to the tactical moves you should master to give yourself the best chance of success in making Oxbridge a reality for yourself.

As important as being curious, dreaming big, working hard, picking your friends wisely, and all the lessons of the past section are (and they really are!), how you approach and execute on the Oxbridge application process is just as important.

For elite sports athletes, training in the gym to increase their strength and stamina is foundational to their on-field success. But equally important is their mastery of their sport, whether that be their racquet technique on the court or their footwork on the running track.

This next section will arm you with the 'racquet technique' and 'footwork' you need to ace the Oxbridge application process.

It's a comprehensive guide covering how good your academic results need to be, how to pick between Oxford and Cambridge, helpful tips on choosing the right Oxbridge college and course for you, how to nail your Universities and Colleges Admission Service (UCAS) application from personal statement to the final interview, and much more.

I'll be focusing on the Oxbridge application process for undergraduate studies, as, speaking from experience, the vast majority of questions I've received about the application process have pertained to this level of study.

However, postgraduates will also find relevant insights from this section – for example, understanding the distinctions between Oxford and Cambridge, guidance for selecting the best-fitting college, tips for crafting a compelling personal statement, and procuring strong reference letters. These are all applicable to both undergraduate and postgraduate candidates. Later in this section, I'll also touch upon the differences and considerations between undergrad and postgrad studies at Oxbridge, having done both myself.

I've done my best to distil the key insights relevant to the Oxbridge application process in this section, but *a word of caution*. Please ensure you also supplement this book with your own research on the process, through official channels and sources, so that you always have the most up-to-date information. The application process is constantly evolving and you should not rely solely on the information in this book as it draws from research I did at the time of writing, corroborated by my own experience.

With that said, let's dive in . . .

13

Academic excellence: A-levels and GCSEs

Oxford and Cambridge Universities search for the biggest and brightest academic minds. Your academic results and achievements are your top priorities, as these relate to admission and selection.

You must ensure that you possess a strong track record of academic excellence to stand a chance of success. The competition is incredibly intense, as you'll be competing against a highly talented pool of applicants with unending strings of top grades and enough A's to fill a dictionary. You'll need to possess tip-top academics as a baseline to be in the running.

Starting with your General Certificates of Secondary Education (GCSEs) or their local equivalent for you (in my case, the Malaysian Certificate of Education [SPM]), you should complete at least eight or nine subjects, achieving straight A's.

You may be able to get away with a B by compensating with very strong A-level results and other achievements at high school, but against a backdrop of thousands of other candidates with straight A's, getting a B for your GCSEs hurts your chances of being admitted. Getting a C or D would be akin to turning up to a Formula 1 race in a Honda Civic and expecting to finish on the podium.

While strong A-level results form the core criteria for admission to Oxbridge, your GCSE performance is also evaluated as a marker of your underlying academic potential, work ethic, problem-solving skills, and motivation to succeed. Your GCSE results provide insights into your broader abilities and serve as a reliable barometer of your potential alongside your A-level results – such as how a good portion of French fries can mean the difference between a good and mediocre meal when having the juiciest, tastiest burger.

As for the 'burger', your A-levels, make sure you take at least *three subjects*. I did four but it's important to note that adding that additional subject probably didn't do too much to increase my chances of getting into Oxford as an undergrad. In fact, in hindsight, I'd advocate quality over quantity – do just three subjects and do them very well.

Because, depending on the subject, conditional offers for Oxford typically range between A*A*A and AAA at A-level, or 38–40 in the International Baccalaureate (IB), including core points. For

Cambridge, conditional offers typically range between A*A*A for most science courses and A*AA for arts courses, or 40–42 in the IB, including core points. So, the bar is extremely high and it's crucial to nail your A-level subjects.

Choose your A-level subjects carefully. They should be subjects that you're passionate about, subjects you enjoy. This will help maintain your motivation throughout the two years of intense study and ensure that securing those A*'s that you need for a competitive university application doesn't feel like an impossible task. Please also make sure you choose your A-level subjects based on the course you want to pursue at Oxbridge as some courses require you to take specific subjects at A-levels, and some A-level subjects such as 'Critical Thinking' are not accepted for certain courses. For example, at Oxford, 'General Studies' and 'Global Perspectives and Research' are not accepted by any course.

While A-level is the most common qualification for which offers are made to students who apply to Oxbridge, Oxbridge does accept other qualifications such as the International Baccalaureate, A-level/Pre-U combination, US APTs or SATs, Singaporean SIPCAL, and French Baccalaureate, among others. You can find the latest on the qualifications accepted by Oxbridge at their official websites.

I'd highly recommend, though, that if you're able to pursue A-levels you do so, as this will be the most straightforward path you can take. If the qualification you've pursued is not accepted in the official Oxbridge lists, then you'll need to undertake further study before you can submit your application.

Finally, while your academic results will form the core of your university application, it's also important to demonstrate your enthusiasm and passion for learning beyond the school curriculum. Oxbridge is looking for well-rounded students who'll contribute positively to intellectual life on campus. To supplement your excellent exam grades, you should show evidence of wider reading around your chosen university subject through reference to this in your personal statement and, during the interview, your ability to discuss your subject more broadly. We'll cover all of this in the upcoming chapters.

14
Oxford or Cambridge? Which to choose?

Oxford and Cambridge share many similarities. Both are elite institutions consistently ranked among the top universities globally. They're both very old institutions with rich histories and traditions. Oxford was founded in 1096 and Cambridge in 1209. They are both collegiate universities, meaning students are members of individual colleges, not just the overall university itself, and they have very similar teaching methods, done through one-on-one or small-group tutorials with the world's best professors in their respective fields. Admission to either Oxford or Cambridge is very competitive and selective, with entry based only on assessments of prior grades and interviews. Both universities have their own esteemed publishing houses, some of the world's most beautiful architecture and, of course, produce leaders and influential thinkers, movers, and shakers in fields such as politics, science, business, and arts, who've shaped and are shaping the trajectory of our world.

But if you're applying for an undergraduate course, it's crucial to know that you cannot apply to both Oxford and Cambridge in the same admission year. You'll need to choose between them.

Given the popularity and competitiveness of the universities of Oxford and Cambridge, it would be an immense logistical challenge for them to evaluate applications properly if students could apply to both universities at once. Each year, Oxbridge receives tens of thousands of applications between them for only a few thousand coveted spots. If students could apply to both in the same admission cycle, it would essentially double the number of applications that each university would need to consider.

More importantly, having applicants commit to a single choice helps Oxbridge ensure their candidates have selected their preferred university, rather than applying to both just to increase their odds. This allows the respective selection committees to make admission decisions feeling more confident that successful candidates have self-selected the university that will give them the best chance of success in launching their careers. (Note: this restriction is not applicable to postgraduate applications.)

With that in mind, it's important to understand the differences between an education at Oxford versus an education at Cambridge, so that you're able to make an informed decision in choosing which one you'd want to commit to.

But first, a bit of history . . .

Oxford is the oldest university in the English-speaking world. It's also the second-oldest university in continuous operation after the University of Bologna (with only eight years between them!). After its foundation in 1096, scholars began gathering at Oxford to study and teach. The institution saw rapid growth from 1167 onwards, when King Henry II imposed a ban on English students attending education at the University of Paris, resulting in many students returning from France. The historian Gerald of Wales lectured Oxford scholars in 1188, and Emo of Friesland, the first known foreign scholar, arrived in 1190. From 1201 onwards, the head of Oxford was recognised as the 'Chancellor', and the university was granted a Royal Charter in 1248 during King Henry III's reign.

Where it gets more interesting is in the founding of Cambridge and the ties Cambridge has with Oxford. In 1209, massive disputes between students and Oxford townsfolk led to some Oxford scholars and academics fleeing north-east to Cambridgeshire, where they established what became the University of Cambridge we know today.

That's right: in a sense, Cambridge was born out of Oxford, a progeny of sorts. (Fun fact: John Harvard, who founded Harvard

University in the United States was a University of Cambridge alumnus – one could then argue Harvard was born out of Cambridge!)

In the Middle Ages, both Oxford and Cambridge gained reputations as centres of learning that drew scholars from across Europe. A friendly rivalry developed between them, resulting in the portmanteau 'Oxbridge' to represent both universities as the twin pinnacles of British higher education, known for their academic excellence, history, and tradition. The two have maintained close scholarly and institutional links as sister universities since medieval times, rooted in their founding principles and rivalry for prestige.

The Boat Race, held annually between Oxford and Cambridge, vividly captures the spirit of competition between the two universities. The race pits the Oxford University Boat Club against their Cambridge counterparts in a stretch of the river Thames located in Henley-on-Thames. You must know that rowing is a quintessential part of the Oxbridge experience. Almost everyone who has gone to Oxbridge has experienced waking up in the early hours of the winter mornings, taking a boat out to the river, eyes still crusty, and then throwing their weight in propelling the boat through the freezing waters. So, the Boat Race is a massive event.

The rivalry between both universities is on full display every year the boats take on the four-mile stretch of the river Thames.

At the Boat Race, and any other sporting competition, such as the Rugby League Varsity Match or the Varsity Polo Match, you may hear Oxonians shout 'Shoe the Tabs!' (derived from 'Cantabrigian'). And the Cantabs reply, 'GDBO!', or 'God Damn Bloody Oxford!'

The rivalry is all in good fun but I often joke that when I knew I was going to Cambridge to do my PhD after my time at Oxford, I didn't have any Oxford friends in my final year at Oxford and didn't have any Cambridge friends in my first year at Cambridge. This is a joke of course!

In terms of comparing both universities, I've compiled the table below to summarise a few interesting statistics and metrics:

Metrics	Oxford (aka 'Dark Blues')	Cambridge (aka Light Blues)
Year founded	1096	1209
Motto	*Dominus illuminatio mea* (translated from Latin to mean 'The Lord is my light')	*Hinc lucem et pocula sacra* (translated from Latin to mean 'From here, light and sacred draughts')
Number of students	26,497 (2022) (circa 12.7k undergraduates, 13.3k postgraduates)	24,270 (2020) (circa 12.9k undergraduates, 11.3k postgraduates)
Times Higher Education World Uni Rankings	No. 1 (2024) No. 1 (2023) No. 1 (2022)	No. 5 (2024) No. 3 (2023) No. 5 (2022)
QS World University Rankings	No. 3 (2024) No. 4 (2023) No. 2 (2022)	No. 2 (2024) No. 2 (2023) No. 3 (2022)
Number of colleges	39	31
Endowment	£8.12 billion (2022; including colleges)	£7.802 billion (2022; including colleges)
Acceptance rates	13.7% (2022)	15.8% (2022)
Notable alumni	J.R.R. Tolkien, Stephen Hawking, Adam Smith, Oscar Wilde, Tim Berners-Lee, Tony Blair, Margaret Thatcher	Isaac Newton, Alan Turing, Charles Darwin, Bertrand Russell, John Maynard Keynes, Niels Bohr

Science versus humanities – the debate

If you've read around the topic of Oxbridge, you might have come across the common perception that Cambridge is stronger for the sciences, while Oxford is better for the humanities. I personally believe there's some truth to this, but the caveat I have is that I also believe the difference to be so marginal it won't make a difference to you as a prospective student at a practical level.

It's interesting to note, though, that in spite of the fact that both universities insist there's no significant difference between them when comparing their strengths in the sciences and the humanities, just looking at their most famous alumni reveals an interesting trend.

Oxford has gained recognition for producing alumni who pursued successful careers in politics, particularly those who studied and graduated with a degree in 'Philosophy, Politics, and Economics'. The university boasts an impressive number of British prime ministers among its alumni. As of 2022, of the 57 British prime ministers, 30 of them were educated at Oxford. In fact, 13 of these hail from a single Oxford college, Christ Church, while Cambridge has produced 'only' 14. Furthermore, Oxford's dominance in this area has been increasing over time, as 13 of the last 16 British prime ministers studied at Oxford compared to none from Cambridge.

On the other hand, when it comes to the Nobel Prize, Cambridge takes the lead, especially in the sciences. As of 2022, the University of Cambridge has seen 121 affiliates honoured with the Nobel Prize, with Trinity College alone contributing 34 Nobel Laureates. In contrast, Oxford has produced 73 Nobel Prize winners. These numbers highlight Cambridge's strength in scientific research and its contribution to ground-breaking discoveries.

But the key question here is, will this make a difference to you as a prospective student?

I don't think so. Both universities are renowned worldwide and rank among the best academic institutions. While it's interesting to consider the contrasting strengths of each university, the opportunities available at both remain exceptional. Which one you choose isn't likely to affect your future trajectory or career significantly.

There are, however, some considerations you should keep in mind when comparing the science and humanities offerings at Oxford and Cambridge. At Oxford, science students are required to choose a specific subject, with little to no flexible science degrees available (joint degrees are offered however). On the other hand, Cambridge is well known for its natural sciences courses, offering a flexible natural science degree that allows students to combine various biological and physical sciences.

In terms of subject rankings, Oxford holds or has held the top spot in the world for subjects such as English Language, Literature, Geography, and Modern Languages, whereas Cambridge ranks first for subjects including History, Mathematics, and Archaeology.

Nevertheless, I maintain that while the science-versus-humanities debate persists, the differences between both universities are marginal on a practical level. Each has produced exceptional alumni in various fields, and their overall academic reputations remain stellar.

Tutorials versus supervisions

A primary factor contributing to the illustrious reputation of an Oxbridge education stems from their rigorous and distinctive teaching methods. Beyond the traditional lectures, classes, seminars, and laboratory sessions common at other universities, Oxbridge also offers its students personalised teaching time with experts in their field. These sessions are very similar across Oxford and Cambridge and the main difference is really only in the name. At Oxford, these are called 'tutorials' and at Cambridge, 'supervisions'.

Tutorials and supervisions make up a large part of Oxbridge's exceptional academic offering. These are personal and intimate teaching sessions where a tutor or supervisor (usually a highly accomplished professor or academic) meets a small group of students to discuss the week's assignment or a particular topic. The number of students is typically fewer than four, but in my experience, they have mostly been two-on-one or sometimes even one-on-one sessions. In these sessions, you have the golden opportunity to partake in energising and mentally stimulating 'intellectual sparring sessions' with your professor or tutor.

Usually an hour in length and once a week with a tutor or supervisor affiliated with your college, the direct personal interaction you get with leaders and experts in their fields offers an immersive and rigorous engagement that greatly cultivates independent and critical thinking. It's an academic apprenticeship of sorts with senior faculty, wherein concepts are explored in greater detail through insightful debate and challenging but supportive discourse, which fundamentally makes the Oxbridge learning experience so renowned.

It's very different from the academic approach you may be used to in school. But if you're a curious, bright, and motivated student, these weekly sessions will be some of the most beneficial sessions you'll ever attend, no question. Tutorials and supervisions are designed to replicate a two-way conversation – the initial Oxbridge interview, where your interviewer is probably assessing how well you'll participate in these later small-group teaching sessions, is probably the closest approximation (but tutorials/supervisions are much less stressful!).

Typically held in your tutor's or supervisor's office in the college or department building, tutorials and supervisions usually start off with a few minutes of small talk to catch up on life updates and how you're getting on with the course content of the past week. Your tutor then dives into a discussion, starting with some basic questions before moving on to harder ones about the chosen topic. Questions will oftentimes be related to the coursework that week.

This is your chance to engage in the two-way discussion, ask questions to gain clarity on concepts you may not fully understand,

and explore ideas to gain a better grasp of the content. It's completely OK not to know all the answers! Interacting with your tutor or supervisor is meant to deepen your learning through questioning and challenging your own preconceptions, while also developing your thinking skills. You shouldn't be afraid to discuss and debate the topics. That's the entire purpose of the sessions. The time will fly by and, before you know it, you'll be wrapping things up with plenty to chew on for the rest of the week.

Oxbridge traditions

Over the centuries, Oxford and Cambridge have developed rich and vibrant traditions that inject wonderful charm into their institutions. From small eccentricities to time-honoured customs to rituals so absurd you can't help but smile, these traditions are what make the experience at Oxbridge so special. In many ways, the frivolity and quaintness of these traditions coupled with the academic rigour of the Oxbridge education is what breathes life into the experience and brings the student communities at each university together.

Let's start with the academic dress at Oxbridge, which is referred to as 'sub fusc'. Sub fusc comes from the Latin *sub fuscus*, meaning dark brown. It's basically an attire consisting of a dark suit, skirt, or trousers with dark hosiery and black shoes, a plain white collared top with sleeves and a white bow tie (you'll notice there's no brown here!). You'll then drape your academic gown (i.e. that billowing black Oxbridge cloak) over this formal attire and sometimes have your mortar board (i.e. that academic cap with a stiff, flat, square top and tassel) clasped in your hands.

You're required to wear sub fusc under your gown for all formal university ceremonies such as matriculations, degree ceremonies, and graduations as well as for Formal Hall dinners, although the exact requirements for the latter may vary by college. Many Oxbridge colleges will require you to wear your gown for Formal Hall at the very least.

A theme you'll see throughout this section on 'Oxbridge traditions' is that Oxford generally tends to be more traditional than Cambridge (it must be because of the hundred-odd years' difference between the two!). And so, as it relates to sub fusc, Oxford requires this formal dress to be worn also when you sit for your end-of-year examinations, whereas at Cambridge, this is not a requirement and you can take your exams arguably in more comfort! It's also worth noting that Oxford tends to be stricter about the wearing of sub fusc under your gown for formal ceremonies and occasions than Cambridge tends to be.

As for the academic gowns themselves, there are some differences between the Universities.

For one, at Oxford, undergraduate gowns are tiered. Most Oxford students taking undergraduate or undergraduate master's degrees will wear the 'Commoners' gown, a sleeveless black gown containing two streamers with square pleating hanging from either side. However, if you're a recipient of a scholarship and/or have excelled in your preliminary examinations at Oxford, you gain the privilege of donning the 'Scholars' gown, a black gown of Russell cord or synthetic material with short open sleeves, the kind you'd imagine draped over young witches and wizards at Hogwarts School of Witchcraft and Wizardry. Candidly, the Scholar's gown served as extra motivation for me to ace my exams – who wouldn't want to feel like a young wizard?

At Cambridge, though, there's no distinction in the type of gowns you wear based on your academic achievements. All Cambridge undergraduates wear a similar gown known as a BA gown (or MA gown if you're doing a Master's degree), a black garment falling just below the knees with sleeves that are open and pointed. It looks more like the Oxford Scholars gown than the Commoners gown. The wonderful thing about Cambridge gowns, though, is that most colleges will have somewhat personalised aspects, minor variations to their pattern such as decorations on the sleeves.

These gowns find the most use during Formal Hall, another Oxbridge tradition and one of the oldest of them all. These are formal dinners, where students don their formal attires to attend a sumptuous three-course meal in their centuries-old dining halls.

The Formal Hall evening usually begins as students gather outside the magnificent wooden doors of their Oxbridge college dining hall, chatting with each other as they eagerly await the feast to come. At around seven o'clock, they enter the hall into a scene that quite frankly could come straight from the pages of the Harry Potter books (the Great Hall of Hogwarts in the Harry Potter movies was filmed in Christ Church, Oxford, after all!).

Flickering candles atop rows of polished wooden tables. Silver cutlery perfectly arranged, from the outer silverware for your starter to the inner silverware for your main course. At the head of the hall, professors and fellows of the college would take their seats on the high table, signalling that you could then take your seat.

Once everyone is seated, a solemn recitation of a Christian prayer commences in Latin. In a college such as Trinity College, Cambridge, this Latin prayer would be punctuated by the sound of a gong. Yes, a gong. And then the dinner would begin.

During Formal Hall, strict dining etiquette is observed. For example, no one should begin eating their meal until everyone around them has been served. The rule of thumb is that the people sitting diagonally opposite you should receive their food before you can start tucking in.

It's also important to know that your bread roll is the one on your left, not right, and you should always remember to use the cutlery from the outside first, working inwards for each course.

Dining etiquette was something I had zero experience of, having grown up in Malaysia, where we enjoyed our food the most by feeling it on our fingers. Formal Halls were always a very interesting experience for me and made me feel quite sophisticated, even if it felt quite awkward in the beginning.

The meal is often accompanied by wine, and, if you're lucky, your college may also serve sherry beforehand and port afterwards.

While you savour your wine, you should remain mindful of the potential threat of 'pennying'.

Dating back to the fourteenth century, 'pennying' is a drinking game at Oxbridge that involves slipping a penny into someone else's drink without their noticing. If you manage to do this successfully, the person who has been 'pennied' must finish the entirety of their wine or drink in their cup or glass.

Similarly, there's another tradition known as 'silvering', where instead of a penny and a drink, if you manage to slip a 5p coin on to another person's dessert plate, the person who has been 'silvered' has to consume their dessert without using any silverware. These traditions are all good fun but if you're ever in the position to penny or silver someone, make sure it doesn't get you into trouble!

Another lovely tradition shared by both Oxford and Cambridge is the tradition of summer balls – highly anticipated events in the academic calendar where students dress up to the nines, indulge in copious amounts of food, drink, and entertainment, and party until sunrise.

The grounds of Oxbridge colleges are transformed into enchanting spaces with elaborate and extravagant decorations. Champagne receptions, food trucks, and open bars, as well as live music, DJs, and performances from popular (and up and coming) musicians are available to all.

At Oxford, these college balls typically take place at the end of the final term. In addition to college balls, Oxford also has Commemoration Balls, which are hosted by certain colleges usually once every three years and are oftentimes white tie. At Cambridge, the balls are called 'May Balls' because they were originally held in May, although they're now held in May Week which is actually at the start of June. Quite confusing, I know.

Based on my personal observations, Cambridge May Balls generally tend to be larger scale. Perhaps Oxford's Commemoration Balls are of the same scale as Cambridge's May Balls, certainly for the more prestigious Cambridge ones such as at Trinity College, St John's College, and Clare College. Regardless, both Oxford's summer balls and Cambridge's May Balls provide a night of revelry and create an atmosphere of celebration, allowing students to decompress after the stressful examination period.

Punting is also a shared Oxbridge tradition and is especially popular during the summer months. Both cities were built near rivers – Oxford has two, the River Thames and River Cherwell, while Cambridge's sole river is the River Cam.

It's on the River Cherwell and River Cam that students and tourists alike would take their punts (which are long boats with a flat bottom) out for a lazy afternoon – the punter pushing a long metal pole against the riverbed to propel the boat forward. Even though punting is popular at both Oxford and Cambridge, they each have their own traditions when it comes to the activity itself. In Cambridge, most punters stand on the till (the flat end of the boat) and punt with the open end forward. On the other hand, it's the tradition at Oxford for punters to stand inside the boat and punt with the till forward.

Having done both, I prefer the Oxford way. It just feels safer to be standing in the boat as opposed to standing on a flat surface of a wobbly punt as you try to push it forward! But when it comes to the scenery itself, I'd say punting in Cambridge is quite a bit lovelier than Oxford. Very few things come close to the beauty of punting on a sunny day along the Backs in Cambridge, seeing the picturesque and charming architecture of some of Cambridge's most renowned colleges, including the iconic King's College Chapel, as you make your way down the river Cam.

From everything I've mentioned so far, to each university's shared tradition in rowing, rugby, and even the annual varsity ski trip, where thousands of Oxbridge students take to the Alps, you can see that Oxford and Cambridge share many similarities in their traditions. However, there are several other traditions that are practised by one and not the other, mostly at Oxford, as the more traditional university of the two.

For one, Oxford has plenty of traditions around their examinations. In addition to having to wear sub fusc, there's an Oxford tradition of pinning a white carnation on your academic wear on the first day of your year-end examinations. You then move onto a pink carnation during your interim exams, and finally pin on a red carnation during your final exam.

I don't know if this is true, but I was told the progressive colour change in your carnation symbolised the blood (sweat and tears) you had to shed to go through the intense examination season.

And after concluding your final exam paper of the year at Oxford, you usually partake in the tradition of 'trashing', which involves being doused by your friends in prosecco, whipped cream, glitter, and other celebratory substances (while you're still in your sub fusc by the way) to mark the end of your exams as an expression of liberation.

There are also other quirky traditions unique to each university, such as the Oxford Tortoise Race and the Cambridge Cardboard Boat Race. As their names suggest, the former is a race involving several Oxford college tortoises (yup, colleges have tortoises) starting their positions at the centre of a large ring of lettuce, and the latter, a race on the river Cam involving boats made out of cardboard, tape, and glue by Cambridge students.

And what about the tradition of 'May Day' at Oxford, where thousands gather at six in the morning on the first of May every year, after a long night of partying, to listen to beautiful Latin hymns sung from atop the Magdalen College tower, welcoming the coming of spring and longer, lighter days. This is then followed by a breakfast of strawberries and champagne.

There are plenty of differences in the traditions at Oxford and Cambridge, with every one of them contributing to the distinct character and atmosphere at each university. You, of course, shouldn't be choosing which university to apply to based on its traditions, but I hope, nonetheless, this section was interesting and helpful in giving you just a little insight on some of the differences.

The final tradition I'll mention is probably one of the most important rules to remember at Oxbridge. So, if there's only one tradition to remember from everything I've shared, just remember that whether you're in Oxford or Cambridge . . . never ever walk on the grass!

Location and environment

With so many things being similar between Oxford and Cambridge, a couple of practical aspects that should influence your choice between the two are their location and environment. The setting of the city, campus atmosphere, and surrounding areas can have a significant impact on your time at university.

Cambridge is the smaller of the two – a picturesque university city where students make up approximately 20 per cent of the population. The university's buildings dominate the compact city centre, lending a beautiful nostalgia to a quaint and laidback town. Thanks to its size, Cambridge feels more intimate than Oxford. And with the River Cam flowing through the city itself, snaking through patches of lush greenery, Cambridge offers a serene natural beauty and idyllic college experience that may appeal more to students who have a penchant for more countryside-type vibes.

Someone once said to me that if Cambridge is a university with a city around it, then Oxford is a city with a university in it. Having been to both, I think this statement captures the differences between both universities very well. Cambridge is a university first and a city second, whereas Oxford is a city first with the university second.

While still small in scale (relative to a megacity such as London), Oxford is larger and more bustling than Cambridge. There are more shops and commercial areas within easy walking distance and Oxford provides a livelier social and nightlife scene with numerous bars, pubs, and clubs. It's a bigger, more energetic city with greater access to urban amenities. For example, one of my favourite things to do when I was at Oxford was to grab an ice cream at 10.30 at night from George & Davis (or more affectionately known as G&D's), Oxford's local and independent chain of ice cream cafes. Or be spoilt for choice between the large number of kebab vans that would mushroom across the city as dusk fell (Hassan's was/is my number one). Things I missed when I moved to Cambridge.

As historic cities, both Oxford and Cambridge offer vibrant culture through renowned museums and galleries. Opened in 1683, Oxford's Ashmolean Museum is hailed as the world's first university museum and Britain's first public museum. It houses huge collections of archaeological specimens and fine art. From Da Vinci to Picasso, it has one of the best collections of Pre-Raphaelite paintings, majolica pottery, and English silver. The Fitzwilliam Museum is Cambridge's analogue to Oxford's Ashmolean. Founded in 1816, it comprises one of the best collections of antiquities and modern art in western Europe, with treasures including artworks by Monet, Picasso, Vincent van Gogh, and Rembrandt. Both universities have numerous other museums, such as Oxford's Museum of Natural History, Pitt Rivers Museum, and History of Science Museum, as well as Cambridge's Sedgwick Museum of Earth Sciences, Museum of Archaeology and Anthropology, and Museum of Zoology.

Famously known as the city of dreaming spires, Oxford's architecture is majestic, reflecting both Gothic and Baroque architectural styles. Oxford colleges with their quadrangles (or 'quads'), arched windows, and cloisters have a gorgeous medieval charm about them. Buildings are often constructed from golden-tinged limestone and the university's iconic buildings such as the Radcliffe Camera, Sheldonian Theatre, Divinity School, University

Church, and Bridge of Sighs all offer a regality and beauty that express the cultural legacy of the university.

Also predominantly Gothic in architecture, Cambridge is blessed with some of England's finest buildings, ranging from the renowned fifteenth-century King's College Chapel to the ornate Victorian facade of Trinity College. There's more open greenery in Cambridge, giving the city and colleges a quieter aesthetic, and college buildings commonly use grey brick and roof slates, creating a lighter tone to Oxford's warmer limestones. The Backs, which is the green land backing the colleges along the River Cam is a gorgeously iconic, postcard-perfect image of Cambridge, which offers a relaxed atmosphere and lovely scenery amid busy academic schedules.

Both universities are gorgeous in their own way, but, between the two, my opinion is that Oxford's architecture is more majestic and impressive as a whole, whereas Cambridge is prettier and offers a more idyllic atmosphere.

When it comes to the university libraries, though, I'd say that Oxford's Bodleian Libraries have an edge over Cambridge's University Library. The Bodleian, as it's sometimes called is one of the oldest and largest libraries in Europe, with a collection of over thirteen million printed items. It stands out both for its historical significance as well as its extensive holdings spanning multiple academic fields. The Cambridge University Library is also highly respected and holds significant collections, manuscripts, and archives. However, as a student who has spent a lot of time at both university libraries, the sheer scale of Oxford's Bodleian is impressive. The Bodleian is so large that it has an underground tunnel connecting the Old and New Bodleian buildings, and originally housed a pedestrian walkway as well as a (now disused) mechanical book conveyor used for book orders!

While both cities are small enough to cover on foot, you'll benefit from getting yourself a bicycle (and learning to cycle if you don't already know how to). The roads are made for cyclists with plenty of cycle paths and so, almost everyone cycles at Oxbridge. I'll say however that with Oxford being a larger, more bustling city than Cambridge, I felt the need to be bolder in navigating the streets and traffic of Oxford.

And as you cycle (or walk) to your lectures at Oxbridge, you'll need to get used to the wet and cold English weather. Don't worry, though – you'll soon adapt and also get used to complaining about the weather in typical English fashion. Even though the climates at Oxford and Cambridge are quite similar, I'd say Cambridge experiences more mist, fog, and wind than Oxford. Cambridge sits on flatter terrain, which means it lacks the barriers to wind that Oxford enjoys due to its relatively hillier landscape.

Finally, the big question. Which one is closer to London?

This is an important consideration because, in the midst of your intense academic schedules, the occasional trip to London on the weekend can mean the difference to your levels of sanity. You'll be happy to know that both cities are very close to London. They are both less than an hour away by train, although travel time from Cambridge is marginally shorter at 45 minutes on the fast train to King's Cross in London, as compared to Oxford's 58-minute train to Paddington in London. Oxford does have a bus service called the 'Oxford Tube' with coaches running day and night every ten minutes.

One more piece of advice

I'm very aware that this is more difficult for aspiring Oxbridge students who live outside the UK, but if you have the means and opportunity to visit Oxford and Cambridge in person, please do, especially during their open days. There's nothing quite like being there in the flesh to learn more about where and what you could be studying for the next three years or more.

Even though attending Oxbridge open days wasn't feasible for me, I know from speaking to many people who've attended them that they're exceedingly helpful. They allow you to explore the historic cities, attend presentations on courses of interest, and ask any question you have on your mind to faculty and current students to gain a deeper understanding of which university would be a better fit.

One of the best parts of Oxbridge open days is that both universities use these events as a means to sell themselves to you. Unlike the rest of your application where you're constantly trying to impress the university to gain entry, it's a refreshing change to have the tables turned, even if just for a day. A dedicated team of people will be on hand to answer any questions you can think of, take you around the colleges, and give tours of all available facilities and even the accommodation on offer.

While open days are traditionally in-person events, virtual open days are quickly emerging as a convenient and accessible alternative. Online open days will mainly consist of lots of virtual tours, plenty of opportunities to talk to professors and current students from the university, and hear detailed advice on preparing for the admission process, all from the comfort of your own home. If you're unable to attend an in-person open day, I'd highly recommend that you attend a virtual one.

Open days are typically held in the summer, between the months of July and September, but you should check for exact dates on Oxford and Cambridge's official websites.

And if you can't attend the open days in-person or virtually, you can still learn a lot about life at Oxford versus Cambridge through resources such as this book and the copious amounts of information available online. Even virtual tours of Oxbridge colleges and departments are accessible through a simple Google search and click of a button!

15
Choosing what to study

Choosing what to study at university is probably the most important decision you'll make regarding your higher education. More important than whether it should be Oxford or Cambridge, or any other question for that matter.

Your choice of subject will not only be what you engross yourself in for at least three years, but will greatly influence your academic path and, very likely, your career path as well for decades to come. Choosing the right course can lead to a richer, more stimulating experience at university and make the most demanding academic programmes feel enjoyable, achievable, and fulfilling. Therefore, it's in your best interest to explore the available options rigorously before you commit to your choice of university course.

Ensure you're fully informed about what your options are and apply restraint if there's an initial choice that seems obvious to you before you've done your research. The most energising and inspiring course could be one you've yet to discover!

In fact, investing time and energy to make an informed decision on what to study is even more important when applying to Oxbridge.

This is because you can apply for up to five courses on your UCAS application but at Oxbridge only one. With so much riding on this single decision, you should feel certain that your selected course is the right one for you.

The first piece of advice I have when selecting a course of study at Oxbridge is an obvious one – you must possess a passion and enthusiasm for it. This is what I call a non-negotiable 'hygiene' requirement. Without this, even if you were able to fool your way into getting into Oxbridge, pursuing your degree would feel like building a brick house on quicksand – you'd have no stable foundation on which to build.

The workload and expectations at Oxbridge are quite a bit higher than at other universities. For example, humanities students may be tasked with writing two lengthy essays per week, while science undergraduates will devote many hours to weekly sessions in the laboratory on top of tutorials as well as lectures.

All this coupled with the fact that the academic terms at Oxbridge are shorter than at other UK universities (eight-week terms at Oxbridge versus twelve-week terms elsewhere) means that the large volume of work is also compressed into a condensed time frame, intensifying the experience even more. Only by loving the material can you thrive under these conditions.

My second piece of advice is that once you've uncovered your passion for a certain subject, still conduct your research into it. In particular, look into the structure and content of the course at Oxford and Cambridge, and consider how these may differ. Studying subjects at degree level can be quite different from studying them in school. By conducting your research, you'll gain a better understanding of how the courses are designed, what topics are covered, and the approach taken by each university. This will help you make an informed decision about whether Oxford or Cambridge aligns better with your expectations and goals for your chosen subject.

One practical thing to be aware of is that while both Oxford and Cambridge offer their students the chance to study a combination of subjects, the structure of their courses can differ.

At Cambridge, their course is called a 'Tripos' and is typically divided into 'Parts'. Each 'Part' lasts one or two years and you take several exam papers to complete them, some compulsory and some optional. Beyond compulsory papers, you may be able to tailor your course to your own interests, and sometimes take papers from other subjects. There are broad courses such as Natural Sciences and Modern and Medieval Languages that allow for specialisation over time, giving you the space and time to explore the breadth of your subject and home in on your interests.

Oxford, on the other hand, offers joint honours courses that allow students to study multiple subjects in different combinations. These courses provide their students the opportunity to explore different subject areas as well as examine the connections between them.

For example, joint courses containing Philosophy could be paired with subjects such as Theology, Psychology and Linguistics, or even Physics. More typically, though, Philosophy tends to be studied as part of the Politics, Philosophy and Economics (PPE) course, one of Oxford's most popular courses that has led to the ascension of many world leaders.

There are also certain courses that are available only at one of the universities. For instance, PPE is only available at Oxford, while Cambridge is the only one of the two universities to offer an undergraduate programme in Education. Make sure you do your due diligence regarding the Oxbridge course you want to go after.

In particular, you'll also want to ensure that you thoroughly research the entry requirements and typical offers for your desired university course. This is because some Oxbridge courses require that you take certain A-level subjects or equivalent qualifications as well as achieve certain grades in specific subjects. This is all to ensure that you're academically prepared for the course material if or when you get to it. For example, if you want to do Mathematics at Cambridge, you're required to have A-levels in Maths and Further Maths.

You should refer to Oxford and Cambridge's official websites for the latest information on which A-level subjects are essential versus helpful versus recommended for your desired course.

My third piece of advice when deciding on your course of study is that you should consider how your future career aspirations align with your chosen course. Certain courses offered at Oxbridge are vocational in nature and directly prepare you for specific careers such as Medicine, Engineering, and Architecture. If you have clarity on what type of career you want to build, you should ensure the degree you're pursuing helps you unlock that career. You'll also benefit from seeking advice from professionals working in the field you want to build your career in to understand the courses they pursued at university as you decide on what course to apply for yourself.

However, if you're unsure of your career aspirations, as I was and so many prospective university students are, you should know that, regardless of the subject, a degree from Oxbridge carries significant weight with all employers. Therefore, I'd go back to my first advice: choose a subject that genuinely interests you and in which you can excel. There are few things with greater academic prestige than a first-class degree from Oxbridge if you can achieve it. Graduating with one of these can act as an automatic qualifier to get your foot in the door at almost any company.

My fourth piece of advice goes back to the open days. Open days remain an invaluable opportunity to immerse yourself in the courses available at Oxford and Cambridge so you gain a taster of what university life could be like. If you're able to take part in them, do make the most of the activities on offer. Attend the course presentations and Q&A sessions. Engage with the professors and current Oxbridge students. Join the departmental tours to get a sense of the learning environment. You'll gain a lot from open days as you assess what subject to study.

OK, with four pieces of advice on what to do, my final one is on what *not* to do. And that is, don't choose your course based on looking at the admission stats.

It's true that different courses at Oxbridge have different admission rates, with some of the toughest degrees, such as Economics and Management at Oxford being as low as 7 per cent. So, I know it can be tempting to choose to study a subject that has a higher acceptance rate. But not only will doing this steer you into a programme you could be less interested in, violating my first piece of advice, but admission stats can be highly misleading.

Admission stats can vary from year to year for a particular course depending on the overall applicant pool quality and other factors outside your control. Multiple factors are considered in a university admission, from your test scores and interview performance to demographic factors and geographic residence, all weighed to varying extents. Stats don't capture trade-offs between this multitude of factors.

Passion for your subject of study is a far more important predictor of success. Not only will it be easier to nail your Oxbridge application process, but you'll have a much better university experience studying something you find truly engaging versus just picking the 'easiest' option to get you in.

16
Picking an Oxbridge college

Unlike most universities in the UK, Oxford and Cambridge have a unique system called the 'collegiate' system. It's one of the most distinguishing aspects of Oxbridge, where both universities are comprised of numerous individual colleges in addition to their academic departments. Oxford has thirty-nine colleges and Cambridge, thirty-one.

As an Oxbridge student, you're not only a member of the university and the department for the course you're taking, but you're also a member of a college.

While the academic departments are responsible for your course content, from the lectures and lab work to your examinations and awarding your degree, colleges play a pivotal role in your university experience.

First, most tutorials and supervisions take place in your college, where, as an Oxbridge student, you receive highly personalised one-on-one or small-group teaching from the best in your field. So, your choice of college will determine the quality of some of your core teaching. Your college tutors are also the ones who oversee your academic progress throughout your studies, further influencing your academic journey.

Second, your college provides a safe environment and warm community in which you can focus on your academics while also enjoying social activities and making the most of your university experience outside the classroom. You get fed by your college, can row for your college, and will party in your college. And as an Oxbridge student, you usually live in college accommodation in the first year of your course, although many students live in college accommodation throughout their entire time at Oxbridge.

From Magdalen College to Christ Church in Oxford, and Trinity College to Peterhouse in Cambridge, Oxbridge colleges take pride in their distinct traditions and even, in some cases, their reputation for the quality of their teaching within certain fields. It's therefore important to consider which college to apply for when you're making your Oxbridge application.

When picking a college, the first thing to check is whether it offers the subject or course you want to study. Most colleges offer most subjects but I'd advise you to look up the course offerings directly on the university or college websites to be sure. Larger colleges will tend to offer a wide range of subjects across many departments, but for less popular subjects, availability may vary more between different colleges.

It's also worth mentioning that while the quality of education you receive won't vary tremendously between colleges, some colleges are known to be more academically inclined than others, such as Merton College in Oxford and Trinity College in Cambridge.

Merton and Trinity have regularly topped the annual college ranking tables for Oxford and Cambridge respectively. The Norrington Table, as it's called in Oxford, ranks Oxford colleges based on their undergraduate students' exam results for a particular year. At Cambridge, their equivalent table is known as the Tompkins Table.

For those outside Oxbridge, these rankings won't mean much. However, a quick online search looking up a college's past placements on the tables offers additional insight (albeit imperfect) into the academic rigour and prowess associated with different colleges, through how their students generally compare in university examinations.

As another minor aside, some colleges are also better known for certain courses due to the professors affiliated with that college.

Jesus College, Oxford, for example has been well regarded for Geography and Churchill College, Cambridge, has built a strong reputation in Engineering. I'm not advising you necessarily choose your college based on this, because part of it is anecdotal and the rest, far from definitive, but it's an additional consideration to have when you're in your research phase.

More objective criteria for choosing a college, however, are its size, location, quality of facilities, and the accommodation on offer.

The size of a college will have an impact on one's university experience. I went to Jesus College, Oxford, which is considered a small college with just a few hundred students overall. I found that because it was a small college, it was much easier to get to know everyone in my year and forge closer connections with all of them, as well as take on leadership positions in college clubs, societies, and sports teams if you wanted to because there's less competition for the roles. I also noticed that one-on-one or two-on-one tutorial sessions were more common at my college being a smaller one than at larger colleges where three- or four-on-one were not uncommon.

On the flip side, student communities tend to be more diverse (at an absolute level just by the law of numbers) and bustling in larger colleges, with greater extracurricular opportunities due to the larger student body. Larger colleges also generally (not always!) have the advantage of providing accommodation for longer durations during your time at Oxbridge and, oftentimes, accommodation that's at or near college grounds, making life more convenient for students.

College location is an important factor for you to consider when picking a college. The decision between a college that's smack in the centre of the city and one that's further out of town, away from the swarms of tourists, can have an impact on your day-to-day life at university.

A city-centre college offers much easier access to shops, restaurants, and entertainment venues, making opportunities for socialising much easier. On the other hand, a college located further out of town, offers a quieter and more peaceful environment that could be beneficial for maintaining focus on your coursework and academics, away from distractions and the tourist hubbub. Living in a less crowded area can also be more affordable, with potentially lower housing costs.

When considering the location of a college, it's essential to think about the proximity to your course department and university facilities such as the university libraries or sportsgrounds. You'll save a lot of valuable time and energy having your college close to these areas, as the majority of the commuting you'll do at university will be to get to your morning lectures, rush to your sports training sessions, and frequent the libraries for a constructive studying environment.

You should consider the college's proximity to the city centre as well. My advice is to find a college that's close to it. Life will be a lot easier as not only will you have greater access to supermarkets, food spots, and entertainment, but there will also be a more vibrant and dynamic student community the closer you are to the centre. Ultimately, though, the choice between a city-centre college and one further out of town depends on your personal preferences and priorities as they relate to your social life, convenience, and academic focus. So, weigh them accordingly when making your decision.

While most colleges generally provide similar facilities and amenities, such as 'Harry Potter-esque' dining halls, lustrous lawns, labyrinthine libraries, and cosy student common rooms ('JCRs', or Junior Common Rooms, for undergraduates, as they're called, and 'MCRs', Middle Common Rooms, for postgraduates), there may also be facilities for which access may vary by college, such as the sportsgrounds, college gardens, and, most importantly, college accommodation.

Access to college accommodation is a really important factor to consider when choosing your college. As already mentioned, some colleges may offer accommodation for the entirety of your undergraduate degree, while others may offer accommodation for only part of it.

And in the cases of colleges that offer accommodation for the entirety of your degree, your accommodation may be located off-site after your first year, potentially distant from the city centre and your department, which was the case for me when I was in my second to fourth year at Oxford.

Some colleges offer rooms with only shared toilets and others have en-suite rooms. Some accommodation is old with creaking wooden floors and separate taps for hot and cold water, some are new with triple glazed windows and underfloor heating. So, it's helpful to enquire about the accommodation you'll have access to when you're in the process of picking your college.

If you have special needs or a disability, you'll want to assess whether the college can provide the necessary support services to accommodate your requirements. If you're able to, I'd recommend you visit the college in person to evaluate its accessibility and support systems for students with special needs or disabilities. This way, you can ensure that the college can offer the assistance you may need throughout your time there.

Some colleges offer a wider variety of scholarships and funding than others. With the increasing costs of higher education, access to funding can be very helpful and, in some prospective students' cases, critical. Wealthy colleges, such as Trinity College, Cambridge, and St John's College, Oxford, provide relatively more college grants and scholarships to help their students manage the high costs of university education. It's worthwhile taking the time to research the types of funding each college has available to their students when in the process of making your choice.

Read different prospectuses and research online. You'll be amazed at how much information is available at your fingertips. And if you can, attend the Oxbridge college open days (yes, I know I sound like a broken record by now) and talk to the current students who are experiencing the college first hand. Ask questions about the college's location within the city, what the college community is like, accommodation options, tutorials/supervisions, and all the aspects I've outlined in this chapter.

Open days also allow you to get a real sense of the atmosphere and aesthetics of the college, which can play a large role in how you feel about it. Personally, I took great pride as an undergraduate in being a part of Jesus College, Oxford, with its charmingly compact yet majestic quadrangles, sixteenth-century buildings, and delightful traditions.

For instance, we had this quirky tradition of popping our cava or prosecco cork, and aiming it at the second quad clock after being 'trashed' at the end of exams. If the cork hit the clock face, it was a sign of good luck and a 'Distinction' to come. I also loved showing off my college to my parents and anyone who visited me, highlighting its rich history and captivating beauty.

If, after all the research you've done, you're still unsure about which college to choose, you can opt for an 'open application', where the university randomly allocates you to a college. It's important to note, however, that this decision is irreversible – you won't be able to request another college down the line if you change your mind.

While an open application to a college may seem convenient, allowing you to focus on other aspects of the application, I'd advise against it. Picking your own college shows you've done your research and thought thoroughly before choosing, demonstrating you've explored various factors such as course offerings, college community, culture, and location.

It also eliminates the chance of your being randomly allocated to a college you may not love or that may be more popular and potentially more competitive to get into. (Even though Oxbridge asserts that choosing a less popular college doesn't increase your chances of receiving an offer, it's still something worth being aware of.)

So, put in the effort. It's well worth it and you'll thank me later.

A couple of fun facts about Oxbridge colleges

Oxford and Cambridge are so tightly linked that most Oxford colleges have a sister college in Cambridge. Commonly paired by similar founding purposes or historical ties, some Oxbridge colleges with the same or similar names are sister colleges. Take for example, Jesus College, Oxford, and Jesus College,

Cambridge, or Magdalen College, Oxford, and Magdalene College, Cambridge.

However, colleges with similar names are not always paired up. St John's College, Cambridge, is not the sister college of St John's College, Oxford, for example. St John's, Cambridge, is the sister college of Balliol College, Oxford, and St John's, Oxford is the sister college of Sidney Sussex College, Cambridge. Arrangements between sister colleges vary from case to case, but they may include reciprocal rights to dine at each other's sister college, book accommodation there while visiting, and invitations to the May balls and college balls.

Another interesting fact is that Cambridge is the only university of the two that still has some women's colleges, while all Oxford colleges are now mixed gender. Murray Edwards, Newnham, and Lucy Cavendish Colleges in Cambridge all admit only women. And so, if you're a woman who prefers single-sex education, you'll need to apply to Cambridge rather than Oxford.

17

The Oxbridge application process

We'll now explore the Oxbridge application process, from covering the logistical steps involved to helpful advice for crafting a compelling application. There's plenty to navigate but the aim is to ensure you maximise every bit of preparation and investment you've done to date, compressing, distilling, and packaging up your experiences and skills into an outstanding application that will ultimately secure you that coveted final Oxbridge interview slot.

The first thing to take note of is that applications to Oxbridge open in June and have a deadline of mid-October each year, which is typically earlier than the deadlines for other UK universities. While I'd advise you to start preparing for Oxbridge as soon as you have a vague idea that it's something you want to aim for (even if it's just through passive preparation, working on things in the background), tactically speaking, I'd recommend prospective applicants begin their preparations at least six to twelve months in advance of the deadline.

The average acceptance rate at Oxbridge is less than one in five for undergraduate studies, so a long enough timeframe to allow you to set yourself up for success through thorough preparation is crucial.

The second thing to know is that applications for both Oxford and Cambridge are done online through UCAS, the Universities and Colleges Admissions Service. UCAS is essentially the company that operates the application process for all British universities and colleges – Oxbridge joined the scheme in 1966.

While both Oxford and Cambridge applications are done online through UCAS, there are some differences in the application procedures between the two.

For Oxford, beyond the online application itself, there are no extra forms to fill in. You may be required to take tests or submit written work (more on this later), but there's no additional form you need to complete.

In the case of Cambridge, after submitting the main application, you're required to complete an additional form known as the 'My Cambridge Application' (formerly called the Supplementary Application Questionnaire or SAQ).

If you're applying for scholarships, however, both Oxford and Cambridge may require additional forms to be completed. It's essential to be aware of the requirements, so be sure to check the official university websites for the latest information.

Written responses – the personal statement

One of the most important parts of your application is your written response or formerly, the 'personal statement'. Your written response or personal statement is a critical gateway to Oxbridge as it's your opportunity to make a lasting impression on your tutors around your credentials, passion, and ability, and, ultimately, your case to be admitted.

I'll share with you my advice and some key things to keep in mind, so that when the admission committees review your application, yours will capture their attention and they'll be compelled to put you through!

The format for written responses changed in 2024 for admissions in 2025. Prior to this, UCAS required what was known as a 'personal statement', which was a free-form essay where you could write about pretty much anything. The format has changed to become structured questions and answers to offer greater support for applicants from different academic backgrounds to structure a coherent application.

While the format is now different from what I and many others were exposed to in the past, the preparation, content, and approach to nailing your written responses remains similar and relevant to the personal statement. For this reason, I'll be referring to the personal statement interchangeably with the new written responses and, for ease and simplicity, will be using the acronym 'PS' to refer to either of them.

As you prepare to write your PS, it's important that you adhere to the UCAS official guidelines, including observing the maximum character limit. This showcases your commitment to submitting a well-structured and thoughtful application, which will reflect well on you. Also keep in mind that your PS will be used for all of your university choices, even for those outside Oxbridge. Therefore, being thoughtful and effective in crafting a comprehensive, cohesive, and impactful narrative is even more important.

To write a compelling PS, let's start with what type of student Oxbridge is looking for.

Oxford and Cambridge are seeking students who are curious, teachable, and mouldable, students who are solution-oriented and independent thinkers who'll thrive in and enrich the academic environment while studying there.

Therefore, when crafting your PS, be sure to keep these qualities in mind, highlighting your academic achievements, character, experience, and broader interests to provide proof and support the narrative that you're everything Oxbridge is looking for.

I think it's impactful to weave anecdotes into your PS, something personal such as an experience or influential figure that sparked your curiosity and passion for the subject you're applying for. I opened my PS sharing the story about *Bill Nye, the Science Guy* and how his experiments drew me into the wonderful world of science and maths, laying the foundations for my interest in engineering. A personal anecdote like this captures the reader's attention, draws them in and creates a meaningful connection between your personal journey and passion for the subject.

Your PS should highlight your academic achievements, extracurricular activities, relevant work experience, and any other experiences that have shaped your interest in the subject. However, I'd advise focusing the bulk of the PS on demonstrating your academic accomplishments and academic curiosity, particularly in subjects related to your chosen course. This could include any academic awards you've received, any independent research projects you've driven, or specific coursework that demonstrates your intellectual curiosity and ability to excel in your field of interest.

As a tactical move, you could even research the course lecture list and use it as a basis to anchor your messaging strategically. This would further signal your interest in the subject and showcase a level of proactiveness others may not have.

And, as you emphasise your academic activities and achievements, don't forget to outline your intentions with your degree and why you believe you're a good fit for your chosen course at Oxbridge. Explain why you're passionate about it, how your interest has developed over time, and what you plan on doing with the Oxbridge experience and degree. This should be a focal point in your PS, as your motivations and goals are just as important as everything you've achieved so far.

I'd dedicate around 15 to 20 per cent of your PS to extracurricular activities if you can. Demonstrating that you're involved in meaningful pursuits outside the classroom will make your application stand out more dynamically.

While Oxbridge primarily evaluates academic talent, proving excellence and high performance in extracurricular activities in addition to your academics shows an all-around mindset for excellence that transcends different environments. It shows that you apply yourself with dedication and high standards to anything you take on. Make a connection and highlight how these experiences have contributed to your personal and academic development.

Always remember that authenticity and self-reflection are essential in a good PS. Reflect on your own personal journey and what you have to offer. What's your unique value proposition and what sets you apart from everyone else?

Perhaps there are personal challenges you had to overcome that have shaped you as an individual. Perhaps you've been inspired to pursue higher education at Oxbridge because you have a deep-rooted desire to make a positive impact on your community or society at large. Whatever it is, be authentically and unapologetically *you*.

Never lie in your PS and avoid overexaggeration as much as you can. Let the PS be a vehicle to represent who you are and shine a light on your unique offering. Use the PS as an opportunity for honest but inspired reflection.

Finally, remember to end your PS responses strongly. A strong conclusion that summarises your key points and reaffirms your passion for the subject leaves a good final impression and ends on a positive note.

As the 'peak-end rule' says, 'an experience is largely judged based on how it's felt at its most intense point (i.e. its peak) and its conclusion (i.e. its end), rather than on the total sum or average of every moment of the experience'. Therefore, ending your PS responses on a high note is incredibly important to create a lasting positive impression regarding your application.

Once you've completed your PS, take the time to proofread, edit, and iterate on it. Pay close attention to your grammar, spelling, and punctuation and ensure your PS flows seamlessly and is easy to follow. The last thing you want is to have a beautifully written PS of substance tarnished by simple errors.

I found that soliciting feedback from my teachers, mentors, and family members provided valuable building blocks in refining my PS. I'd advise you to do the same. And do leave enough time to iterate and iterate and iterate on it so that the result is a PS that's concise, effective, and polished.

Creating a compelling and impactful PS is crucial for increasing your chances of gaining admission to Oxbridge. By applying the advice I've shared, you can showcase to Oxford and Cambridge why you're the student they're looking for. Focus on highlighting what makes you unique, share your passion for the subject you wish to study, and mention personal experiences that have motivated and shaped you. Most importantly, write authentically from your core and own your story, and you'll stand out from the crowd.

References

References are an important part of the Oxbridge application process. While not the most important factor, they supplement a student's profile with additional (more unbiased) angles that can help strengthen an application to secure the Oxbridge interview. It's therefore worthwhile ensuring you have them in order. This section sets out some tips and advice for maximising the effectiveness of your references.

First, what exactly is a reference?

A reference is a letter of recommendation written by a teacher, tutor, or other educational referee who knows the student well, especially from an academic point of view. It's completed online as part of the UCAS application and gives crucial additional insight into a candidate's character, capabilities, and potential beyond their grades and PS. References are seen as a more neutral and less biased assessment than if a candidate were to evaluate themselves. As such, admissions tutors tend to place a bit more weight on references than, say, the PS, although the PS is still incredibly important!

The first thing you need to do as a candidate is to select your referee wisely. This is probably the most important advice I can give here. A good referee can mean the difference between a compelling, enthusiastic reference, and a vague, nonchalant one.

It's important to select a teacher or tutor who can speak of your academic achievements, motivations, and potential in a detailed and positive way based on firsthand experience. Make a list of potential referees and shortlist teachers from whom you've received mentorship on assignments or projects, and whose classes you've performed well in.

Once you've identified your best referees, reach out to them well in advance to respectfully and courteously ask if they'd be happy to write a recommendation letter for you. Nine out of ten times, they'll be more than happy to.

Use this outreach and interaction to build rapport with them and get them vested in your application. Explain to them why you'd really appreciate their recommendation, why you've approached them and not other teachers or tutors, and share with them what you have under your belt that makes you a prime candidate for Oxbridge.

Once they agree, let them know what details you'd like them to consider including in their references and endorsement. They'll appreciate your making the process that little bit easier for them too as they support your goals.

A good teacher reference is specific – one that avoids generalisation. Admission tutors want as much specific information as possible about a candidate's performance and what makes them unique. Generic, vague statements such as 'She is an outstanding student' or 'He is intelligent' without providing examples is not good enough.

Good references about you as a candidate include facts such as your academic ranking in class or your success in specific projects and assignments compared to your peers. They're specific to you and clearly outline what exactly sets you apart.

Good references also avoid lukewarm statements. In the sea of applications where countless of them will be glowing reviews, having a lukewarm statement in a reference can be a severe disadvantage. A good reference expresses enthusiasm around your academic performance, using specific examples of your achievements to support the claims. Even if you may not be the best in class, one can still spin a positive and energetic reference focusing on what you do particularly well.

Finally, the reference is an excellent place to provide further context around any extenuating circumstances, especially if you as a candidate have faced challenges academically.

Nobody is perfect and there may be areas of an application where you've failed academically to meet the typical requirements.

Encourage your teachers to provide context around these aspects in their reference letter. Admission tutors do take extenuating circumstances into account when evaluating applications.

Admissions tests

Besides the PS and teacher references, you may be required to take an admissions test as part of your Oxbridge application process. The test will depend on the course you've applied for and can be in written, verbal, or practical form. The purpose is to assess your academic ability and, ultimately, your suitability for your chosen course, as the test results will have a direct impact on the outcome of your application.

At Oxford, the admissions tests are typically written aptitude tests conducted before the interview. They provide the admissions office valuable insight into a candidate's capabilities and limitations, and are required for many Oxford courses. Be sure to look into whether your course requires an admissions test and what it entails to prepare adequately. Most tests are computer-based and it's important to know that registering for the test is not automatic. So, ensure you follow the process carefully and register as soon as you find out, even if you've not yet submitted your UCAS form.

At Cambridge, on the other hand, the admissions tests more commonly take place on the day of the interview. However, pre-interview tests, known as 'Pre-Registration Assessments', are also held for specific subjects such as Economics, Law, and Natural Sciences. Be sure to confirm what your course requires and whether you need to register for these tests on your own.

You should know that you're not expected to answer every question correctly, as these assessments are designed to challenge you. Some strong applicants may even struggle to complete the test in the allotted time and almost no one achieves full marks.

To enhance your preparation for your admissions test, it's helpful to be aware of the average scores achieved by candidates invited for an interview and those who go on to receive offers. These scores may vary each year, so stay updated and aim to surpass the average scores to make your application more competitive.

Additionally, be mindful that test formats may also change, which may render past papers irrelevant. Familiarise yourself with what's required and ensure you prepare yourself sufficiently to nail these tests.

Some examples of tests include Oxford's Biomedical Admissions Test (BMAT), English Literature Admissions Test (ELAT), and Mathematics Admissions Test (MAT), as well as Cambridge's Engineering and Science Admissions Test (ESAT), Test of Mathematics for University Admissions (TMUA), and National Test for Law (LNAT). You can get the latest on admissions tests by visiting the universities of Oxford and Cambridge official websites.

For many subjects, submitting written work may also be a requirement. This may involve submitting one or two pieces of writing that were completed as part of your regular schoolwork.

Check with your course department and college whether they require additional written submissions before your interview, as this can vary based on individual circumstances. If required, take the time to choose your strongest example and solicit advice from your teachers and mentors in the process. You may even consider writing something new tailored to Oxbridge's request. Whatever you choose, ensure it's your most compelling piece that has been marked and revised thoroughly so you're submitting the best possible version.

Finally, if English is not your first language, you'll need an English language qualification at a level that depends on your specific course requirements. In particular, you'll need an adequate level of spoken and written English if you're invited to the Oxbridge interview stage, where a strong grasp of the language will be crucial to your ability in demonstrating your intellectual capacity.

This is a nice segue into the next chapter. With the Oxbridge application process now well covered, it's time to address the Oxbridge interview stage. In the next chapter, I'll equip you with valuable tips and tools to impress your interviewers and conquer the final hurdle of the application process to, finally, secure your coveted spot at Oxbridge!

18
The interview

The interview stage is the final hurdle separating you from your spot at Oxbridge. If you manage to make it this far and receive an invitation to be interviewed, it means you've successfully crafted a compelling application that robustly captures your past achievements, present motivations, and future potential. Importantly, it also means you likely have what it takes to study at Oxford or Cambridge. You should be very proud. But . . . it's not over yet. You still have to seal the deal!

Delivering a strong interview performance is crucial and will have a direct impact on the outcome of whether you get a congratulatory offer letter or a consolatory email from Oxbridge.

If you've nailed the application using the advice and tips I've shared, you should expect to receive a letter typically around December, inviting you for an interview. The interviews themselves usually take place around mid-December and January, and it's important to note that they cannot be rearranged or rescheduled around you. Therefore, you'll need to make sure you can attend them or make yourself available for them.

Generally speaking, the interviews will be held at your first-choice college, although subsequent interviews at other colleges may also be scheduled. At Cambridge, it's more common for applicants to be interviewed by only one college, whereas at Oxford, applicants more commonly face interviews from both their first-choice college and a second college. Sometimes, even a third.

The composition of the interview panel may vary, ranging from a single interviewer to a small group, depending on the college and course you've applied for.

If you're an international applicant, you're sometimes given the opportunity to visit the university for the interview, have the interview online, or attend an in-person interview in your home (or nearby) country. I did mine in Malaysia many years ago but, from what I can tell, these overseas interviews are becoming less common than they used to be.

Each interview is unique and depends on many factors, including, but not limited to, the subject and college you've applied for. They can be challenging, nerve-wracking, and intimidating, especially if you're unsure of how best to prepare for them.

So how should you prepare for the Oxbridge interview? I have seven top tips to help you prepare effectively for the day.

1. *Reflect on your motivations.* The first step in preparing for the interview is to reflect on why you're applying. Remind yourself of your motivations and aspirations and take note of what attracts you to Oxbridge as well as why you're passionate about your chosen course. Write these down so you can persuasively articulate your enthusiasm for and commitment to Oxford or Cambridge during the interview, demonstrating your genuine interest in the subject and the university itself.

2. *Familiarise yourself with the course.* Showing a deep understanding of the course you've applied for is crucial and will be something that your interviewers will test you on when they meet you. Therefore, you should take the time to review the course syllabus, paying particular attention to the modules and content you could cover in your first year. Doing this type of research ahead of the interview will not only demonstrate your genuine interest, but also showcase your proactiveness in engaging with the course content and give you plenty to talk about when delving into the subject matter.

3. *Know your written responses or PS like the back of your hand.* As mentioned in the previous chapter, your written responses (or PS) are a critical component of your application. They'll very often serve as a starting point for the interview, especially when your interviewer is trying to break the ice. Ensure you have a strong grasp of what you've written as interviewers may refer to specific points or examples in your PS. And be prepared to elaborate on them confidently and authentically. Printing out your written responses and thoroughly reviewing them ahead of the interview is good practice.

4. *Practise mock interviews.* Interviews can generally be awkward and unsettling if you lack experience in doing them. But, like anything else, practice makes perfect, and practising mock interviews is a great way to build your confidence and refine your interview skills. You could seek the help of your teachers, mentors, or alumni of the universities, and there are lots of mock-interview services for Oxbridge applications you can find online these days (although they can be very expensive and, in my opinion, are unnecessary). Utilise what you can to become more comfortable with the interview as a concept/process and learn how to navigate tricky questions without losing your nerve.

5. *Gather relevant work samples.* If you've submitted any work as part of your application, such as essays or projects, make sure you have copies of them at hand. And like your written responses or PS, you should be very familiar with their contents and be prepared to discuss them, from explaining your thought process to talking through any challenges you faced.

6. *Stay up to date with current developments.* Oxbridge interviewers often expect candidates to showcase a broader interest in and engagement with a subject beyond what's taught in the classroom. Keep abreast of the latest developments and news related to your chosen field of study. Being able to discuss your subject intelligently in the context of what has happened in the world recently will seriously elevate the impression you make on your interviewer and show that your passion and curiosity extend beyond the confines of the academic syllabus.

7. *Sharpen your subject knowledge.* As for an exam you're about to take, you should revise your subject syllabus ahead of the interview so that you'll go into it in tip-top condition academically. During the interview, you'll often be posed questions around topics related to the course you've applied for. Hence, you'll utilise the knowledge you have around the subject to work through these questions with your interviewer. Spending the time to sharpen your

subject knowledge will ensure you're fighting fit going into the interview.

Oxbridge interviewers are, more often than not, tutors at the universities themselves. Ultimately, they're looking for candidates who have excellent analytical skills and logical thinking, underpinned by insatiable curiosity and a willingness to learn.

The interview serves to replicate the tutorial or supervision setting – as mentioned earlier, Oxbridge's highly personalised weekly teaching sessions – and your interviewers are using the interview to assess how you might perform in these sessions with them and other academics.

During the interview, keep these pointers in mind:

- *Be teachable.* The most helpful piece of advice I can give you is to be teachable during the interview. Admissions tutors are looking for candidates who are open to learning and receptive to new ideas. They don't expect you to know all the answers – if you did, you wouldn't need to be studying at Oxbridge! Instead, showing clear logical thinking in breaking down the questions, while demonstrating a deep desire to learn is exactly what your interviewer is looking for. Show true curiosity and enthusiasm towards your subject and the interview questions you're posed.

- *Think of the interview as friendly intellectual discourse.* Your interviewers are not there to catch you out. They genuinely want to get to know you and see how you think through challenging questions or scenarios. Approach the interview as an opportunity to showcase your ability to engage in discussions thoughtfully, logically, and collaboratively with your interviewer.

- *Showcase your strong knowledge about your subject.* Your interviewers will expect you to have a solid foundation in your chosen subject. Showcase your strength in the subject by being specific in any of your examples and elaborate on your answers confidently instead of providing just brief responses. If you're able to, make real-world connections to the topic you're discussing (perhaps books or news articles you recently read) and try to use proper vocabulary and terminology associated with the subject. And, whatever you do, avoid regurgitating information – your interviewers don't want to hear rehearsed answers. Instead, they want to see your ability to think critically and thoughtfully by applying your knowledge of the subject to new situations.

- *Don't be afraid to ask questions.* In addition to showcasing your ability in the subject through your answers, consider the power of good questions as well. Asking insightful and thoughtful questions is a great way of demonstrating your knowledge, interest, and passion. Even just asking clarifying questions is an elegant way of manoeuvring out of situations where you don't immediately know the answer to your interviewer's questions. The interview is not an interrogation – it's a chance to engage in a meaningful two-way conversation. So, remember to ask questions if you need clarification or want to delve deeper into a topic – your interviewer will respect you for it.

- *Take your time.* It's important not to rush your response. It's perfectly OK, and in fact recommended, to take a few moments to gather your thoughts in formulating your answer. Your interviewers are interested in your thought process and ability to reason, so it's never a bad thing to take a bit of time before answering if this allows you to articulate a coherent answer or thought process.

- *Show confidence and enthusiasm.* Confidence is key during the interview. Maintain good eye contact, speak clearly, and use pauses to pace your speech. Relax, be yourself, and let your genuine passion and enthusiasm for your subject naturally shine through in your body language and vocal tones.

The final question you may have about the interview is what you should wear. Like any interview, it's important to strike a balance between comfort and a polished appearance. Choose a smart outfit that reflects respect for the occasion, while ensuring that you feel comfortable and confident in what you have on.

With the tips in this chapter, you have everything you need to outperform at the interview stage. Give everything you have and leave nothing on the table. After all, this is your final hurdle.

19

Undergrad versus postgrad

I spent eight years of my life at Oxbridge – four as an undergraduate at the University of Oxford and four more as a postgraduate at the University of Cambridge. Having spent almost a decade at Oxbridge spanning both undergrad and postgrad studies, there are some clear differences between the two I thought would be worthwhile covering as a brief aside in this book.

It's important to note that these are my personal observations and reflections, and the undergrad/postgrad experience can vary tremendously depending on a multitude of factors, not least the subject you choose to do, whether it's a master's degree or a PhD, and so on. This chapter is therefore not intended to be a comprehensive comparison of the undergrad and postgrad experience at Oxbridge. Some of what I'll outline is anecdotal and may be biased by my own experience. Nevertheless, I hope it will still be helpful to you.

The first difference I noticed was the distinct nature and level of competition in admission between an undergraduate versus a postgraduate course at Oxbridge. Undergraduate programmes at Oxbridge tend to be extremely competitive due to the large number of applicants vying for entry. Half the qualifying student population in the UK applies to read an undergraduate degree at Oxford and the other half, Cambridge. So, getting admitted represents a huge achievement against the crowded field.

The nature of competition for postgraduate programmes is different. Postgrad programmes tend to have a smaller pool of applicants. Hence, admission rates are generally higher than for undergraduate courses. This is of course a generalisation as there will be specific postgraduate courses that have lower admission rates than some undergraduate programmes, but on average, this remains my observation. One could imply from this that it's easier to get into Oxbridge for postgraduate compared to undergraduate studies. And in the most simplistic of terms, I'd probably agree.

However, I don't think it would be fair to make this claim universally. For one, while the pool of postgraduate applicants will generally be smaller, the quality of candidates will tend to be higher on average. This is because postgrad applicants tend to be higher-achieving undergraduates who've made the decision to further their education.

What I can attest to, however, is that the academic intensity of my undergraduate degree was quite a bit higher than my postgraduate

PhD experience. The condensed terms, extensive coursework, and regular exams made the undergraduate experience incredibly demanding.

In contrast, the PhD programme felt to me more like a nine-to-five job, with more loosely defined academic terms and fewer time constraints. I'd continue working during the Christmas, Easter, and summer holidays for my PhD, which allowed me to free up my regular evenings and weekends from work, alleviating the intensity.

Of course, a PhD programme is different in nature from an undergraduate programme. There's a lot less studying and a lot more research. If you were to pursue a taught master's degree at Oxbridge, it would be more similar in intensity to the Oxbridge undergraduate experience, albeit condensed into a single year (or two). So, you always have the end in sight, which may make it easier to weather the barrage of coursework when it comes.

The experience also differs greatly between an undergraduate and postgraduate education because of where you are in your own journey of personal growth. As an undergraduate, you're earlier on in that journey and in the process of experiencing life. Everything feels new, whether that be living on your own for the first time, discovering the highs of drinking for the first time, or even falling in love for the first time. Your undergraduate experience will involve many more 'firsts' as you discover who you are and what you want in life. In contrast, as a postgrad, you've usually matured to some extent and will approach your university experience with a different perspective and mindset.

You may be thinking at this point, 'The differences Julian's covered so far are subjective and how I experience these things will depend on my individual circumstances.'

And I'd respond, 'I agree with you . . . But that's exactly the point.'

So, with so much up to personal circumstances, what's objectively different between being an undergrad versus a postgrad Oxbridge student?

One aspect that's objectively different is the tutorial or supervision system. As you now will know, the tutorial or supervision system is a core aspect of your education as an undergraduate student at Oxbridge, involving small-group learning sessions with your professor or tutor.

As a postgrad, you're not given tutorials or supervisions in the traditional Oxbridge sense. You'll have regular meetings for example with your research advisors, some of which may be quite 'tutorial' in nature, but they're done in a way that's common among most research degrees anywhere, rather than being tutorials specific to Oxbridge's undergraduate programmes. In some cases, as a postgrad student, you may be the one giving the tutorials or supervisions to the undergrads instead!

The application process for postgraduate studies at Oxbridge is also slightly different from the undergrad process. First, it will differ depending on whether the postgrad degree is a taught programme, such as an MBA, or is research based, such as a PhD.

While applications are done online, just like the undergrad application process, taught master's require a personal statement, whereas research master's or PhD applicants need to write a research proposal. If you're applying for a research-based postgraduate programme, you'll need to identify faculty members whose work relates to your proposed area of study, and contact them to discuss the possibility of their becoming your supervisor. While not mandatory, having the support of a pre-selected supervisor will significantly strengthen your application. Conversely, a taught master's requires less focus on identifying a supervisor, as coursework and internship experiences are prioritised.

If you need to find a supervisor, it's worthwhile checking with your undergraduate professors at your current university if they know anyone at Oxford or Cambridge and can make an introduction. This was exactly what I did in my final year at Oxford, and the contact my Oxford professor gave me in Cambridge ultimately became my PhD supervisor there.

Additionally, unlike the undergraduate application process, where you need to choose between Oxford or Cambridge, you can apply to both universities for your postgraduate studies. The restriction applies only to undergrad and not postgrad applications, which is great if you remain undecided.

There are a few nuances that make the undergraduate experience different from the postgraduate experience at Oxbridge. It isn't straightforward to compare the two directly.

Irrespective of whether it's an undergrad or postgrad degree you're after, having an Oxbridge degree will open many doors. While an undergraduate degree from Oxbridge may carry more initial prestige, a postgraduate degree signifies a higher level of education and academic dedication.

Having 'Oxbridge' on your resume in either form is an impressive feature and will be a boon to your future endeavours, whatever they may be.

20
Financials

My parents always told me that going to university is an investment. I never fully appreciated what they meant by this when I first saw the astronomical costs of pursuing higher education.

The high university fees, especially as an international student coming from a developing country with a much weaker currency, such as Malaysia, made no sense to me. You could use that money to start your own business or choose to save it and join the workforce out of high school instead.

But with the benefit of hindsight, I now see how powerful a good university education, especially from Oxbridge, can be.

The amount I paid in fees and living expenses while I was at Oxbridge was paid off within just a few years after graduating, and I continue to enjoy accelerated financial returns in my career to this day. All because of the opportunities I uniquely have access to as an Oxbridge alumnus – from the greater awareness of and outreach from high-paying industries to the camaraderie felt between Oxbridge alumni excelling in their own careers, which results in mutual support.

Nevertheless, the financial considerations for pursuing an Oxbridge education are substantial. You must be as informed as possible about this before going into the process.

First, tuition costs for both Oxford and Cambridge undergraduate degrees are approximately the same. Although, Oxford is slightly more expensive if you're an international student.

At the time of writing this, it costs roughly £9,000 per year for UK and Ireland students for both Oxford and Cambridge. At Oxford, international-student fees start at around £28,000, and at Cambridge, £24,000, and they can go as high as £55,000–£70,000 a year if you're studying Medicine.

And this covers tuition fees only. It doesn't cover living expenses and college fees, which go on top. It's a lot of money but it's worth noting that the study costs for both Oxford and Cambridge are generally cheaper than those for top US universities such as the Ivy League ones.

A few common scholarships the UK offers for university education are the Chevening scholarship and Commonwealth scholarships.

Oxbridge also offers a range of scholarships and college bursaries to help with the high costs of tertiary education. The financial support offered by Oxford and Cambridge is not the same and it's worthwhile researching what each university has available on its official website.

Examples of scholarships provided by Oxford:

- Crankstart Scholarship for UK students studying their first undergraduate degree and with an annual household income of £32,500 or less.
- Hill Foundation Scholarship for students from the Russian Federation wishing to study for a second undergraduate degree.
- Palgrave Brown Scholarship for students from certain Eastern European countries who need financial assistance.
- Reach Oxford Scholarship for students from low-income countries.
- Dr Ateh Jewel Foundation Awards for UK students of Black African or Black Caribbean heritage, who are from disadvantaged backgrounds.
- Oxford Centre for Islamic Studies (OCIS) Undergraduate Scholarship for UK students from a Muslim community.

Examples of scholarships provided by Cambridge:

- Cambridge Trust Scholarship for undergraduate applicants with overseas fee status studying any subject.
- Cambridge Thai Foundation Scholarship for Thai students studying any subject at any degree level.
- Hill Foundation Scholarship for students from the Russian Federation wishing to study for a second undergraduate degree.
- Prince Philip Scholarship for Hong Kong students studying any subject.
- Rowan Williams Cambridge Studentship for students from unstable or conflict-ridden areas who may have faced discrimination, persecution, suffering, violence, or human rights abuses.
- Beacon Scholarship for students from Kenya, Tanzania, or Uganda applying for an undergraduate degree.

As you can see, a wide range of scholarships and bursaries is available to help any qualifying student benefit from the prestigious Oxbridge education. These do change from year to year, so be sure to keep updated through Oxford's and Cambridge's official websites.

While pursuing a university education at Oxbridge requires substantial financial investment, as an alumnus of both universities, I believe the returns are well worth it.

Investing in Oxbridge is investing in yourself and you're well worth investing in!

Part 3

Closing Remarks

21
Nailing the offer

It was an unremarkable Friday, a week and a bit before Christmas. I'd just taken a cold shower and the sun had sunk beneath the horizon. I decided to check my email and at the top of my inbox sat an unread message from Jesus College, Oxford.

I nervously hovered my cursor over it and clicked to open its contents. And there it was – an official letter confirming a conditional offer for me to read Engineering, Economics and Management at the University of Oxford.

To say I was elated would be an understatement. I can hardly recall many more times in my life when I experienced such an overwhelming surge of emotions. I'd just achieved my ultimate dream!

It's a feeling I hope you'll get to experience too, now that you're armed with the wisdom, tools, advice, and tips in this book. I'm confident that if you put into practice everything I've set out, you'll be able to realise your dream of getting into Oxbridge (or any other top university you've set your sights on).

But getting the offer is not the end. Getting into Oxbridge is.

And so, the next few months are absolutely critical to ensure you meet every condition set out in your offer. These next few months are the final mile of your marathon. You've worked so hard to get to where you are, but you need to cross the finish line and bring the prize home. You need to nail the offer!

My Oxford offer was conditional upon my obtaining A2 Level grades of AAA, including an A in Mathematics and an A in Physics, and I spent my remaining months working hard to ensure that I didn't squander this golden opportunity.

If and when you receive your Oxbridge offer too, make sure you don't become complacent or lose focus. I've seen people who've failed to meet the conditions of their offers and it devastated them. Their offers were essentially rescinded and everything they'd worked so hard for felt in vain.

It's important to remember that getting an offer is just another step in the road – an important step, but just a step, nonetheless.

The hard work continues after receiving your offer to ensure you meet the conditions laid out. Oxbridge has admitted you based on your accomplishments and future potential. It's now up to you, by securing the grades you need, to prove you can perform at the exceptional level expected of Oxbridge students.

Organise your study schedule, seek support from your teachers and mentors, utilise all resources available to you and approach your final exams with full dedication and focus. Practise past papers, look after your physical and mental well-being, stay motivated and from the outset stamp out any inklings of complacency.

You have to earn the distinction and prestige that an Oxbridge degree can confer. Stay focused and run that final mile of your marathon with utmost determination and resilience.

Remember – the final mile is where champions are made. This is a life-changing opportunity you've worked tirelessly for and now is not the time for distractions or self-doubt.

You've proven your capabilities to the admissions committee, and now it's time to prove it to yourself.

Nail the offer and bring it home.

22
Final thoughts

Getting into Oxbridge or any top global university is a wonderful dream to have, especially as a kid. As you've read in this book, it involves investing in yourself to grow to match the size of the opportunity. It requires you to commit to personal development and consistent improvement so that you're able to step up to the plate when the moment comes. And, like anything of substance that's worth doing, it isn't easy and requires a great deal of effort.

The foundations in Part 1, to me, are the most important chapters in this book. They contain deep wisdom that transcends the Oxbridge ambition and permeates every facet of living a fulfilling, rewarding, and interesting life.

Being curious, dreaming big, and keeping an open mind. . . Excelling in what you love, picking your friends wisely, and ignoring what other people think of you . . . Being disciplined, working hard, and focusing on learning . . . Being present, positive, humble, and hungry. . . These are all lessons applicable not just to the star Oxbridge candidate, but also to any individual who seeks a happy and fulfilled life, with or without an Oxbridge degree.

Part 2 covers the practical aspects of getting into Oxbridge. These are more tactical in nature to ensure you're able to navigate the application process, make the right choices to shape the experience, and pull together the most compelling application to secure a place.

From understanding the academic requirements, to deciding between Oxford and Cambridge, to choosing a subject and a college, Part 2 covers everything you need to know including the rigorous application process, crafting strong written responses or a PS and references, and nailing the final hurdle, the interview. I even covered the financial aspects for you, my personal reflections on the differences between an undergraduate and postgraduate education, and the importance of running that final mile to achieve the grades required to secure your Oxbridge offer.

I hope this book has given you everything you need and more to realise your dreams. The reward for all your effort in securing a place at either (or both!) of the world's most prestigious institutions is immense. Oxbridge will open many doors for you, which can be as life changing for you as it was for me.

Having said all that however, I think it's important to emphasise that getting into Oxbridge is not everything. Life doesn't stop when you get into Oxbridge, nor does it stop if you don't get in.

Many people fall into the trap of obsessing over a prestigious university education to the degree that it becomes all-consuming, and where failing to get in shatters their world as well as their self-esteem. This sadly misses the point of dreaming big to get into Oxbridge. A dream this big should never be reduced to just getting an offer letter. It's about the journey you've taken to better yourself and transform your life so that the offer letter is a mere by-product of a greater picture.

So if, even after all you've done to invest in yourself, you don't get that coveted offer, still celebrate the personal growth you've driven for yourself. Remember that you're much bigger than any accomplishment and far, far, far more important. Catch yourself before you become so overly obsessed with the Oxbridge dream that you feel it's starting to define you.

As mentioned in Part 1, just give everything and expect nothing in the pursuit of your Oxbridge dreams. If you achieve them, fantastic. If you don't, so what? You're not defined by your achievements, trophies, titles, or positions in life. You're still worthy and success will follow you in other ways if you continue to prioritise investing in yourself.

And if you're a parent reading this book, with the aspiration of seeing your child or children gain admission into Oxbridge, please go about it the right way. While it's natural to want the best for your children, it's important to remember that, ultimately, their dreams and aspirations should be their own.

Don't force your dreams on them or live vicariously through your children's accomplishments. Gently guide them to see the potential benefits and opportunities of a world-class university education and cultivate their hunger for excellence from within. Help them recognise the advantages of learning from some of the brightest minds in their respective fields and the potential doors that a good education could open in terms of career prospects.

But maintain an environment that allows your children to explore their own interests and set their own goals. I was incredibly lucky to grow up in an environment where neither my father nor my mother ever imposed strict expectations on me, academically or otherwise. They always gently guided me but left me to make my own decisions. I only wish for more kids to have parents such as mine.

Ultimately, the decision to pursue an Oxbridge education should be made by aspiring individuals themselves. It's their journey and they should feel empowered to own their dreams.

So, if you've set your sights on Oxbridge, I wish you the very best of luck. I hope this book has given you the valuable insights, strategies, and inspiration you need to make your dreams a reality. Believe in yourself and I hope you find yourself roaming the hallowed grounds of Oxford and Cambridge in the not-too-distant future!

Photographs

My well-worn college hoodies from Oxford and Cambridge.

Memories of my first Oxford 'bop' or 'Big Organised Party'.

Discovering snow for the first time in Oxford as a Malaysian.

Examination Schools, University of Oxford, where all my examinations took place.

A Polaroid photo of me after my final exam at Oxford (note the red carnation).

Being 'trashed' – what liberation!

Signing the student register to become an official member of Clare College, Cambridge.

Gathering for our matriculation photo at Cambridge.

Punting along the river Cam on a beautiful, sunny day.

An impressive entry at the Cambridge Cardboard Boat Race.

Breakfast of strawberries and champagne, an Oxford tradition on 'May Day' after a full night of partying.

Childlike glee at St John's College, Cambridge, on a winter's day.

A bit of mischief at the Christmas formal dinner in Cambridge, also known as 'Bridgemas' (at Oxford, it's known as 'Oxmas').

Formal Hall dinners were always a highlight. Here, I'm with the committee members of the Cambridge University International Students' Union, where I served as Vice President.

G&D's ice cream, Moo-Moo's milkshake, and (the original) Ben's Cookies – the holy trinity of Oxford's sweet treats.

Graduation day at Oxford.

Graduation day at Cambridge.

Dressed to the nines here for Trinity's and Clare's May Balls.

A night of revelry and great memories at Trinity's 150th anniversary May Ball.

The moment I submitted my PhD thesis after three-and-a-half years of hard work.

Visiting the grand dining hall of Christ Church, Oxford, upon which the design for the Hogwarts Great Hall in the Harry Potter films was based.

The second quad of my Oxford college, where you can see the large clock (at the upper right-hand corner of the photo). At the end of exams we'd aim our prosecco/cava cork at the clock. If the cork hit the clock face, it was a sign of good luck and a "Distinction" to come.

My final day as an Oxbridge student.

Below are some cherished snapshots I took of the University of Oxford while studying there.

The view of the Radcliffe Camera from inside Exeter College.

Christ Church on a lovely day.

The intricate and majestic ceiling of the Divinity School.

All Souls College (left) and a solemn Christmas tree at the Bodleian Library (right).

And some of my favourite of Cambridge.

Punters enjoying the Backs during golden hour.

The ornate fountain of Trinity College, Cambridge, on a clear summer's day.

The view of Clare College Bridge, which I crossed a hundred times to get to college.

The magnificent ceiling of King's College Chapel (left) and the Mathematical Bridge of Queen's College in the snow (right).

Sources

Official Oxford and Cambridge websites:

- https://www.ox.ac.uk/admissions/undergraduate
- https://www.undergraduate.study.cam.ac.uk

Crimson Education Blog:

- https://www.crimsoneducation.org/uk/blog/oxford-vs-cambridge/

Oxbridge Applications:

- https://oxbridgeapplications.com/blog/oxbridge-applications-a-level-guide

Amber Student Blog:

- https://amberstudent.com/blog/post/the-difference-between-oxford-and-cambridge

The Profs:

- https://www.theprofs.co.uk/student-resources/university-applications/undergraduate/how-to-get-into-cambridge/
- https://www.theprofs.co.uk/student-resources/university-applications/what-to-do-if-you-dont-meet-oxfords-entry-requirements

Meet University Blog:

- https://meetuniversity.com/blog/the-10-hardest-oxbridge-degrees-to-get-accepted-on/

The Student Room – Uni Guide:

- https://www.theuniguide.co.uk/advice/ucas-application/what-do-i-need-to-get-into-oxford-or-cambridge-straight-a-s
- https://www.theuniguide.co.uk/advice/ucas-application/oxford-or-cambridge-choosing-which-university-to-go-to

The Complete University Guide:

- https://www.thecompleteuniversityguide.co.uk/

Cambridge Coaching Blog:

- https://blog.cambridgecoaching.com/admissions-5-things-to-know-about-getting-into-oxford-and-cambridge

About me

I'm Dr Julian Tan L. Y. and I reside in London, working as a senior executive in sport, media, and entertainment. I've held senior positions at Formula 1, Flutter Entertainment Plc, Boston Consulting Group, EQT Group, and so on, and was named 'Leader Under 40' by the Leaders Sports Awards in recognition of my contributions to global sports and entertainment.

I grew up in Malaysia and at the age of seventeen moved to the UK to study engineering at the University of Oxford. I graduated with First Class Honours and was the top scholar of my college. I then pursued my PhD at the University of Cambridge, where I researched carbon fibre laminates in collaboration with Boeing and Mitsubishi. I was one of the fastest students in my lab to complete their PhD at three years and four months, publishing my work in prestigious academic journals, including the Royal Society, which has previously featured authors such as Isaac Newton and Stephen Hawking.

I'm one of only a few Malaysians ever to achieve the 'Oxbridge double' and it has given me the wonderful life I have.

It's a life full of opportunities, complete financial security, a profoundly expanded outlook, and an unwavering sense of confidence – a life I wish everyone to have. I trust this book will not only be informative for aspiring Oxbridge students but also inspire anyone who wants to achieve their dreams.

Made in the USA
Middletown, DE
12 October 2024